# COACHING IN EDUCATION

# The Professional Coaching Series

## Series Editor: David Lane

Other titles in the Series

*The Art of Inspired Living: Coach Yourself with Positive Psychology*
by Sarah Corrie

*Business Coaching International: Transforming Individuals and Organizations*
by Sunny Stout Rostron

*Integrated Experiential Coaching: Becoming an Executive Coach*
by Lloyd Chapman, with contributing author Sunny Stout Rostron

*Coaching in the Family Owned Business: A Path to Growth*
edited by Manfusa Shams and David A. Lane

# COACHING IN EDUCATION

## Getting Better Results for Students, Educators, and Parents

Edited by

*Christian van Nieuwerburgh*

**KARNAC**

First published in 2012 by
Karnac Books Ltd
118 Finchley Road, London NW3 5HT

British Library Cataloguing in Publication Data

A C.I.P. for this book is available from the British Library

ISBN 978 1 78049 079 3

Edited, designed and produced by The Studio Publishing Services Ltd
www.publishingservicesuk.co.uk
e-mail: studio@publishingservicesuk.co.uk

Printed in Great Britain

www.karnacbooks.com

# CONTENTS

.

*ACKNOWLEDGEMENTS*                                               ix

*ABOUT THE EDITOR AND CONTRIBUTORS*                              xi

*SERIES EDITOR'S FOREWORD*                                       xvii

### PART I: COACHING IN EDUCATIONAL CONTEXTS

CHAPTER ONE
Coaching in education: an overview                               3
   *Christian van Nieuwerburgh*

CHAPTER TWO
Coaching and mentoring for educational leadership                25
   *Christian van Nieuwerburgh*

CHAPTER THREE
Coaching in primary or elementary schools                        47
   *Mary Briggs and Christian van Nieuwerburgh*

CHAPTER FOUR
Coaching in secondary or high schools                            63
   *Christian van Nieuwerburgh and Jonathan Passmore*

CHAPTER FIVE
Mental toughness and its role in the                          75
development of young people
    *Peter Clough and Doug Strycharczyk*

CHAPTER SIX
Coaching to improve teaching: using the                      93
instructional coaching model
    *Jim Knight*

CHAPTER SEVEN
Positive education programmes: integrating coaching         115
and positive psychology in schools
    *Lisa Suzanne Green, Lindsay Gregory Oades,*
    *and Paula Lesley Robinson*

CHAPTER EIGHT
Coaching for parents: empowering parents to create          133
positive relationships with their children
    *Agnes Bamford, Nicole Mackew, and Anna Golawski*

CHAPTER NINE
Creating coaching cultures for learning                     153
    *Christian van Nieuwerburgh and Jonathan Passmore*

PART II: CASE STUDIES

CHAPTER TEN
Coaching in primary schools: a case study                   175
    *Neil Suggett*

CHAPTER ELEVEN
Coaching students in a secondary school: a case study       191
    *Christian van Nieuwerburgh, Chris Zacharia,*
    *Elaine Luckham, Glenn Prebble, and Lucy Browne*

CHAPTER TWELVE
Coaching staff in a secondary school: a case study          199
    *Loic Menzies*

CHAPTER THIRTEEN

Coaching in higher education: a case study                205
    *Bob Thomson*

*INDEX*                                                     215

*To my wife, Cathia, and my son, Christian, who bring out
the best in me, and to all those who bring out the best in others.*

*ACKNOWLEDGEMENTS*

I am grateful to everyone who provided support and encouragement in this undertaking. The authors of the various chapters are all experts in their respective fields and have been incredibly generous with their support and time. Their thinking, experiences, and commitment to coaching in education has been inspirational and has shaped my understanding of this important field. Many of these authors have become good colleagues and friends.

The School of Psychology at the University of East London has been a wonderful place in which to research and discuss coaching. I am particularly grateful to Mark Davies, Aneta Tunariu, Ho Chung Law, Julia Yates, and William Pennington for their commitment and support for the coaching psychology programme. I learn the most when I am with the students on our MSc Coaching and Coaching Psychology programmes. Thank you for your challenging questions, insightful comments, and your passion for coaching. It is a privilege to support you in your journeys to become coaches!

One perk of my professional life is the opportunity to visit schools and educational organisations. I would like to record my gratitude to every school, college, and university that has allowed me in to see the way they work. On the whole, I am encouraged and re-energised by what I see: hard-working, committed, and passionate professionals working with students who have enormous potential.

I am lucky to be part of a growing international community of university-based academics who are interested in the practical application of coaching within educational settings and I am genuinely grateful to everyone who is working in this field. Jim Knight is doing wonderful work at the University of Kansas and has been incredibly generous with his knowledge and expertise. Tony Grant and Suzy Green at the University of Sydney have been a source of constant admiration and encouragement. Everyone at Karnac has been immensely helpful and encouraging, making the writing process very pleasurable and stress-free. I am particularly grateful to the series editor, David Lane, for his calm and thoughtful approach to this project.

My almost (?) obsessive interest in the field of coaching in educational settings must exact a toll on those who provide me with the most love, support, and encouragement: my family. I am blessed with the most wonderful wife, Cathia, who puts up with my obsession because she is similarly caught up in the world of academia. She is a constant source of love and support. My son, Christian, inspires me through his love of learning and way of being. He even humours me by occasionally asking for some coaching! My mother, Tsuyu Tsuchida, continues to be a model of generosity and resilience. I am also grateful to the Jenainati family for embracing me as one of their own.

**Agnes Bamford** delivers coaching courses in schools to parents, teachers, and students. She also delivers various types of business coaching and group facilitation in organisations. She is a postgraduate qualified coach with an MSc in Business and a degree in Psychology. Agnes is also a qualified UK teacher. As a working mother of three children, Agnes can relate to the challenges and emotions faced by most parents. Agnes has experienced the difference parent coaching can make for parents and families, and she believes strongly in empowering parents to generate the relationship with their children that they dream of having.

**Mary Briggs** is an Associate Professor in the Institute of Education at the University of Warwick. She teaches on a number of different education courses with a specific research interest in mentoring and coaching, mathematics education, leadership, and assessment. Her coaching research has focused on children's perspectives as well as those of adults working in schools, and she has presented this work in the USA and Spain. Mary has published widely across these areas of interest. She has worked in a wide range of settings, including children's homes, special schools, primary schools, and universities.

**Lucy Browne** is currently a trainee educational psychologist and completing her Doctorate in Education and Child Psychology at the University of East London. She has previously completed a Masters degree in Enabling Learning, and also has a Bachelors degree in Psychology. Lucy has previously worked as a Looked After Children Education Adviser, multi-agency team co-ordinator, and Intervention Manager in a secondary school. She is passionate about inclusion and supporting young people with social, emotional, and behavioural difficulties, and supporting staff to work with vulnerable young people.

**Peter Clough** is a Chartered Psychologist and is a senior lecturer at the University of Hull. His main research interests are in performance in high-pressure environments. He is co-developer, with Keith Earle, of the mental toughness model and of the MTQ48, the mental toughness questionnaire. This has now found widespread application in education with both young people and staff. Peter's consultancy experience is wide-ranging and includes implementation of assessment and development centres, workplace counselling, employee surveys, leadership development, and assessment. Peter's Masters degree (Sheffield University) is in Occupational Psychology. He earned his PhD at Aberdeen University.

**Anna Golawski** is a postgraduate qualified coach who has a down to earth, objective, and practical approach. She has a natural ability to build trust and rapport with her clients, which helps them to get the most from their coaching sessions. She started coaching over eight years ago as part of her MBA, and has enabled numerous clients to achieve their goals and ambitions. Anna specialises in coaching for education, corporate and not-for-profit sectors, primarily focusing on coaching skills for parents, teachers, and work–life balance programmes. She brings with her a wealth of talent and experience gained over the past fifteen years in business, including Harrods, IBM, and Rolls Royce. Anna writes coaching articles for magazines and is a business mentor for the Prince's Trust. She has written a book on coaching skills for parents, which is due to be published this year.

**Suzy Green** is a Registered Clinical and Coaching Psychologist and a Member of the Australian Psychological Society, based in Sydney. She is a leader and pioneer in coaching psychology and positive psychology, having conducted a world-first study on evidence-based life coaching. Suzy has been the recipient of a Positive Psychology Fellowship Award and has been published in the *Journal of Positive Psychology*. Suzy is an Adjunct Lecturer in the Coaching Psychology Unit, University of Sydney, and teaches Applied Positive Psychology. She is also the co-founder of the Positive Psychology Institute providing clinical, counselling, and coaching services for individuals and organisations. Suzy is also a resident expert for *Australian Women's Health Magazine*, and writes a regular "stress-less" column.

**Jim Knight** is an internationally renowned thinker and writer in the field of coaching in education. As a research associate at the University of Kansas Center for Research on Learning, he has spent over a decade studying instructional coaching, and has written several books and academic articles on the topic. Jim has consulted and presented in most US states, in Canada, Japan, Australia, and the UK. He has a PhD in education and has won several university teaching, innovation, and service awards. He writes the popular radicallearners.com blog.

**Elaine Luckham** spent seven years teaching English as a Foreign Language in the Far East, Italy, and the UK, before settling in the UK and embarking on an NLP training course. She then moved into state education, working for the past four years as Higher Education Adviser for a large community college in Kent. Combining a long-standing interest in all aspects of personal development and the professional imperative to apply coaching principles at work to help students progress, Elaine recently embarked upon an MSc in Coaching at the University of East London. In addition, Elaine provides leadership development and training for her organisation, as well as individual staff coaching.

**Nicole Mackew** has worked in the corporate sector for more than twenty years, in sales and commercial roles. She studied for a post-graduate Certificate in Coaching in 2004, initially specialising by providing maternity coaching. Her approach encouraged women to return to work with confidence, be effective in the workplace, and manage the additional pressures of parenthood. This was followed by further studies in parent coaching. She has delivered courses in both the private sector and for local authorities. Nicole is passionate about improving the quality of life for working parents. When delivering programmes, she consistently seeks evidence of employees' improved capabilities within their workplace, as well as their experiencing a better quality of life at home. Nicole is part of a family of four, married, with a teenage stepson and young son.

**Loic Menzies** is Director of LKMco. His interest is in how society nurtures children and young people into adulthood. He works with schools and youth organisations to provide training, improvement services, and project development. He bases his academic and policy research on this work. He has worked across the youth and education sectors, first as a youth worker and with youth charities, and then as a Teach First teacher. He gained his experience of leadership in a challenging secondary school, which became the fifth most improved school in the country.

**Lindsay Gregory Oades** was a clinical psychologist before becoming interested in coaching and positive psychology. Lindsay developed this interest in mental health service provision before applying it to management and, more recently, education. Lindsay is currently Director of the Australian Institute of Business Wellbeing at the Sydney Business School, University of Wollongong. He recently co-authored the article "Towards a positive university" in the *Journal of Positive Psychology*, applying positive education in the tertiary sector.

**Jonathan Passmore** is one of the UK's leading coaches. He is a chartered occupational psychologist, an accredited AC coach, a coaching supervisor, and fellow of the CIPD. He has wide business consulting experience having worked for PricewaterhouseCoopers, IBM Business Consulting and OPM, and as a chief executive and company chairman in the sports and leisure sector. He is the author of thirteen books in the field of coaching and organisational change. With an international reputation for excellence, Jonathan is a consultant, executive coach, and facilitator working across the UK, Europe, and the USA.

**Glenn Prebble**. Having graduated from De Montfort University as a geography and PE teacher, Glenn taught in three schools before being appointed Assistant Headteacher at Sittingbourne Community

College in Kent. In 2010, he achieved SEAL (Social and Emotional Aspects of Learning) hub status for the college, which allowed him to develop the principles of emotional intelligence across a number of schools in Kent. He has recently worked with undergraduates from the 14–19 PGCE at Christchurch University, Canterbury to support their professional development in emotional intelligence. A nationally renowned field hockey player, Glenn played for England from the age of fifteen through to under-21 level and has coached the Bedfordshire County Men's 1st XI since 1999.

**Paula Lesley Robinson** is a registered psychologist with twelve years' experience at senior management level. Paula combines her practical business knowledge with her experience within the profession of psychology. Paula's current PhD research is on "mental fitness" and creating a scientifically valid and reliable measure to supplement measures of physical fitness. Paula is co-founder and owner of the Positive Psychology Institute, which provides clinical, counselling, and coaching services to a broad range of individuals and organisations.

**Doug Strycharczyk** is the CEO of AQR, a leading test publisher. Doug's expertise includes developing psychometric tests. He has played a key role in developing the MTQ48 and ILM72 tests, as well as in the creation of a number of organisational development and leadership development programmes. He now works with schools, colleges, and universities to develop programmes and approaches which attend to student performance, wellbeing, engaged behaviour, employability, and transition. This work takes him to countries on all five continents. Doug has co-authored, with Peter Clough, *Developing Mental Toughness*, published by Kogan Page (2012). Doug holds a first class honours degree in Economics. He is a Fellow of the CIPD and a member of ILM.

**Neil Suggett**, CBE, has worked as a teacher, head teacher, inspector, and leadership developer. He is a practising leadership coach and has delivered coach development programmes locally, nationally, and internationally. He has been a research associate at the National College, has worked as a National Leader of Education and is currently a Visiting Fellow at the London Institute. He was awarded the CBE in 2010 in recognition of his services to education.

**Bob Thomson** is a learning and development adviser at the University of Warwick, where he acts as an internal coach and facilitator. He runs the Warwick Leadership Programme and the University's Certificate in Coaching and Mentoring and Diploma in Coaching. He also supervises coaches and mentors, and acts as a mediator. He is the author of two books published by Chandos Publishing: *Growing People: Learning from Day to Day Experience*, and *Don't Just Do Something, Sit There: An Introduction to Non-directive Coaching,* which has been translated into Chinese with the title *Modern Midwifery*.

**Christian van Nieuwerburgh** is a highly sought-after executive coach, researcher, educational consultant, and keynote speaker with significant leadership experience in the public sector. He currently divides his professional time between three engaging and rewarding roles: Programme Leader for the MSc in Coaching and Coaching Psychology at the University of East London, where he heads one of the world's leading university-based postgraduate programmes in coaching psychology. His particular area of expertise is in the impact of coaching within the education sector. www.uel.ac.uk/psychology/coaching; Chief Executive of the International Centre for Coaching in Education. Through this organisation, Christian delivers consultancy, training, and executive coaching to clients in the UK and internationally. www.icce.uk.com; Executive Coach for West Midlands Councils. Christian is an executive coach and facilitator of peer supervision working across a number of public sector organisations in the West Midlands. www.wmcouncils.gov.uk/coachingpool. Christian has enjoyed a richly diverse career. He held senior marketing and business development roles in a number of organisations within the hospitality and fast moving consumer goods sectors in the Middle East, a marketing role for the Royal Shakespeare Company, and senior management roles in two highly rated local authorities in the UK.

**Chris Zacharia** is a Chartered Educational Psychologist with over eighteen years experience of working in the UK and Australia. He is a certified coach, NLP practitioner, and member of the BPS. Specialisms include coaching young people, families, and senior managers in schools. He particularly enjoys training young people and professionals in using coaching, NLP, and other change technologies. In 2003, Chris was awarded the Gold Quality Service Award for his contribution to the production of the CD, *A Pocket Full of Posies*.

# Coaching in education: a need met

Coaching has a long history in education, but its scope has increased considerably in recent years. Its research base is growing, as are the theoretical underpinnings which inform practice. This book looks at both of these, but has as its focus practical applications in a variety of educational settings from primary to higher education and with students, parents, and staff.

It provides a comprehensive introduction to the area. We are delighted to welcome it as the latest in our Professional Coaching Series. The editor and contributors have explored the area through the evidence base, but have always placed that in the context of case examples and stories. This enables the reader to gain a real sense of the concerns practitioners face as they grapple with the issues within education to which coaching offers possible solutions.

As the editor makes clear, the past decade has seen a substantial increase in coaching activities throughout the educational sector. He argues that coaching has a significant and beneficial role to play in challenging students and educators to achieve more of their potential. Coaching, as a person-centred approach, supports the idea of learning as personalised and challenging. It provides a perspective on learning as a personal engagement with change.

Its importance in education in the UK was marked by its endorsement by the Department for Education and Skills in 2003 as one process available to school leaders engaged with continuous improvement strategies. This was paralleled by increasing acceptance of its role in education in the USA. So, although the field is comparatively young, the growing evidence base has received official endorsement, but, more importantly, practitioners using the approach have found that it works for them. In part, this might be because it is a means to develop emotionally intelligent leadership. Given the perceived shortage of aspiring leaders in education, coaching also provides the safe space in which such potential can be explored and nurtured.

While much of the work in the field has focused on secondary and further education, the editor has sought contributions from across the spectrum. Education in its many forms is represented. This provides an important counterbalance to much of the existing literature. How we support children and parents matters, as well as recognising that we need to attend to the needs of staff and administrators. However, the different contexts represented each present their own risks and the contributors do not shy away from addressing them.

In looking at primary education, the contributors of Chapter Three raise issues such as fewer staff needing to cover a broad range of functions, and the impact of disagreements in a small group are discussed. The position of children and the limited range of choices they have, including in setting an agenda for coaching, are addressed. As the contributors state, the key issue appears to be who is driving the agenda for coaching. If coaching is about self-determination, coachees must select their own goals and have a sense of self-agency.

In considering coaching in the secondary school, Chapter Four outlines the number of different purposes it might fulfil. Coaching programmes offer the opportunity to support students and enhance educational attainment. The issue of resilience is addressed. The use of coaching is explored as a means to address the problem of bullying and stress. This is placed within the context of how secondary schools could use coaching with staff to build a learning culture within their school. Clearly, if coaching is able to address this range of concerns, it has the potential to make a positive difference. How it makes that difference and the impacts of it are examined in this chapter.

The issue of resilience or mental toughness is taken up in Chapter Five. The concept itself is explored and four areas are elaborated:

control, challenge, commitment, and confidence. Through examination of research and case studies, it is argued that mental toughness is strongly correlated with performance, wellbeing, aspirations, positive behaviours, completion/drop-out rates, and employability. The role of coaching in building mental toughness is fully elaborated.

From consideration of the position in UK schools, we turn to the USA. Interest in coaching has, as the contributors make clear, exploded in the USA. Coaches have been hired across many states, districts, and schools. Yet this has often happened without considering the principles, actions, and contextual factors that have been found to increase coaching success. The issues this raises are fully explored in Chapter Six.

The role of positive psychology in coaching in schools is explored in Chapter Seven. Positive psychology has increasingly been seen as playing a core role in coaching (indeed, the first book in the Karnac Professional Coaching Series was based in this discipline). However, for its impacts to be sustained, it must be used as part of a positive education strategy rather than being one of numerous initiatives that are not integrated. Achieving this is explored.

Parents are key members of the educational community, and coaching courses for parents have been increasingly provided within schools. A key to this provision is that the coaches are not experts on parenting, but, rather, focus on the use of powerful questions to enable parents to understand their own role and support the belief that their children can succeed. By helping parents improve communication with their children, the experience at home and in school is improved. The contributors of Chapter Eight argue that the results of parent coaching link directly to the five *Every Child Matters* outcomes. They are useful tools for local authorities, schools, and educational organisations for adapting work with parents across all walks of life. Parental coaching has also found its way into corporate initiatives to support parents who are employees as part of a diversity or corporate social responsibility agenda. The outcomes, it is argued, increase employee engagement and satisfaction.

The chapters so far have demonstrated the value of coaching within different educational sectors. So, how do you create a coaching culture to enhance learning? This topic is addressed in Chapter Nine through looking at the journey to create a learning organisation in which coaching is an effective part. This provides a valuable framework in its own right, but is also an excellent introduction to the case studies that comprise Part II of the book.

Hayes Park Primary School has become widely known as the "coaching school". Coaching has become a fundamental part of how they operate. The case study in Chapter Ten illustrates how coaching is being used on a day-to-day basis. The key is that it forms part of their philosophy of shared responsibility for leadership.

The next case study (Chapter Eleven) looks at coaching students in a secondary school. It is based on a collaborative research project between Sittingbourne Community College (with 1,000 + students), educational psychologists within Kent, and the University of East London (UEL). It started as a project for raising attainment using coaching. Coaching was seen as consistent with the school's general ethos, which valued the student voice and saw leadership and responsibility as fundamental aspects of a student's education. Coaching took its place alongside the Social and Emotional Aspects of Learning (SEAL) strategy. This embeds emotional intelligence within the curriculum. Post-sixteen students were given three days of training and then invited to coach younger students (Year 11). The results showed positive effects on both the coached and those coaching.

A project within a London secondary school is investigated in Chapter Twelve to see how coaching techniques could contribute to staff development. The outcomes of the project show that coaching can be both a useful skill for supporting colleagues and to develop the wider culture of the school. It promotes a learning culture and is enjoyed and welcomed by staff.

In Chapter Thirteen, the final case study looks at higher education and the use of coaching at the University of Warwick. The aim of the scheme (which was established in 2006) was to create partnerships, outside the normal line management relationship, that enable one person to help another to enhance their performance, learning, or development. The issues relating to training and supervision and the difficulties they present are covered in the chapter. The view of the author is that the higher and further education sectors present similar issues to coaching elsewhere. Clients are helped to look at how they manage themselves, relationships to colleagues, and their performance.

Coaching is taking hold in education in the UK, USA, Australia, and elsewhere at all levels. It is proving to be a valuable tool to enhance learning. This book address the concerns that are raised when introducing coaching and provides a clear indication of how to address them and build a positive framework that delivers value to all stakeholders within the educational community.

I am delighted to introduce this latest addition to the Professional Coaching Series as one that will support you and your organisation to enhance the learning experience for everyone, staff, students, and parents alike. Coaching is a means to harness the energy and positive thinking within your organisation. This book shows you how to do so. I am sure that you will both enjoy it and gain practical insights into the exciting development that is coaching in education.

David A Lane
Professional Development Foundation

# PART I

# COACHING IN EDUCATIONAL CONTEXTS

# CHAPTER ONE

# Coaching in education: an overview

*Christian van Nieuwerburgh*

C oaching is already having an enormous impact on education. From the UK to the USA and Australia, the use of coaching is increasingly being seen as a useful intervention to support students, teachers, and administrators. In this book, we recognise and celebrate the ways in which coaching is already making a difference in educational organisations and offer ways in which schools, colleges, and universities throughout the world can further exploit the potential of coaching and mentoring.

For students, mentoring and coaching opportunities include providing peer support to fellow students to enhance examination results and improve academic skills. This type of coaching can also reduce stress whilst improving social and emotional skills. For teachers, educational leaders, and administrators, coaching and mentoring can help with transitions into new roles. Coaching is also used effectively to enhance teaching skills and drive up performance in educational organisations. The aim of this book is to support you to implement and embed effective coaching approaches and programmes into your educational organisation. To do this, we will consider coaching approaches and experiences from the UK, the USA, and Australia.

The focus is on the practical application of coaching approaches and the growing body of research into this area. We aim to provide the evidence-based, theoretical context for coaching in education while also proposing a number of specific, education-friendly coaching models that have been tried and tested in schools, colleges, and universities. Throughout, the approach is accessible and practical, using case study examples, diagrams, and stories from practice.

## The new millennium

The past decade has witnessed a notable increase in coaching-related activities in educational contexts. Head teachers, principals, and university administrators have started to introduce coaching along-side more traditional continuing professional development activities. Coaching in education can take many forms and has an impact on a broad range of potential beneficiaries. This includes staff (such as teachers, school leaders, and university lecturers), students, and other stakeholders (such as parents, governors, and members of the community). Training in coaching skills now forms part of the professional development for school leaders in the UK and has been recognised as the new leadership skill for educators in the USA.

## Key questions

If our aim is to harness the potential of coaching within educational organisations, a few questions need to be addressed first of all. As you will see throughout this book, coaching has enormous potential to make an important contribution to learning and development in its broadest sense.

## What is the purpose of our educational systems?

To make the most of coaching interventions in educational organisa-tions, it seems necessary for educational leaders, policy-makers, administrators, and practitioners to agree on the purpose of educa-tion. In other words, in order to address the issue of how coaching might support our educational systems, we need to be clear about what that system is trying to achieve. And yet "what is the purpose of education?" is a very challenging question that has been, and continues to be, fiercely debated. Traditionally, schools and colleges were often seen simply as places for the transfer of knowledge. However, it has also been recognised that "the business of education is not only intellectual. There must be an opportunity for the exercise of responsible choice . . . and also for the acquisition of skills" (Jeffreys, 1971, p. 118).

At a global level, the Universal Declaration of Human Rights (1948) proclaimed that "education shall be directed to the full development of human personality and to the strengthening of respect for human rights and fundamental freedoms" (Article 26). In the USA, the explicit mission of the Department of Education is to "promote student achievement and preparation for global competitiveness by fostering educational excellence and ensuring equal access" (2010). In the UK, the Department for Children, Schools, and Families (DCSF) stated that

> ensuring every child enjoys their childhood, does well at school and turns 18 with the knowledge, skills and qualifications that will give them the best chance of success in adult life is not only a right for each individual child and family, it is also what we must do to secure the future success of our country and society. (2009)

If we accept that modern education is about learning as well as encouraging young people to exercise "responsible choice", that it should support the "full development of human personality" mentioned in the Universal Declaration of Human Rights, that it has a role to play in social justice and equity, and that it can influence the future success of people and nations, then it becomes clear that coaching has a significant beneficial role to play through supporting, encouraging, and challenging students and educators to enjoy their educational experiences and achieve more of their potential.

On the other hand, an influential American educationalist, John Dewey, argued strongly against the notion of education having a purpose:

> education as such has no aims. Only persons, parents and teachers, etc., have aims, not an abstract idea like education. And consequently

their purposes are indefinitely varied, differing with different children, changing as children grow and with the growth of experience on the part of the one who teaches. (1916, p. 125)

Coaching, through its person-centred learning approach, is a powerful way of supporting all those persons involved in education. It supports the notion that learning should be personalised and changing. Dewey's approach proposes that both the "student" and "teacher" develop and grow through the learning experience. As we will see later, this is a key principle of coaching in education.

## What is coaching?

Much of the recent scholarly work about coaching has focused on executive coaching (e.g., de Haan, 2008; Dembkowski, Eldridge, & Hunter 2006; Hawkins & Smith, 2006; Passmore 2010; Peltier, 2010). In these texts and others, there have been numerous attempts to define the practice.

- "Coaching is a robust and challenging intervention, is results driven, delivers tangible added value, is typically a short-term or intermittent engagement and enables the attainment of high standards or goals" (Grant, 2007, p. 23).
- "The aim of coaching is to improve the coachees' performance by discussing their relationship to certain experiences and issues" (de Haan, 2008, p. 5).
- "Coaching could be seen as a human development process that involves structured, focused interaction and the use of appropriate strategies, tools and techniques to promote desirable and sustainable change for the benefit of the coachee and potentially for other stakeholders" (Cox, Bachkirova, & Clutterbuck, 2010, p. 1).
- "Empowering people by facilitating self-directed learning, personal growth and improved performance" (Bresser & Wilson, 2010, p. 10).

It is fair to say that there is still ongoing discussion and debate about an agreed definition. There seems to be broad agreement that coaching is about helping a person to achieve their goals or improve their performance through structured one-to-one conversations.

## Coaching in education

"Coaching in education" is a relatively distinct area of work that has been growing over recent years, starting in the early 2000s. Similarly to other sectors, educational organisations have used the term "coaching" quite loosely, to refer to a number of widely differing approaches.

In the UK, the emergence of coaching was supported by the publication of a Key Stage 3 National Strategy booklet in 2003 (Department for Education and Skills (DfES)). *Sustaining Improvement: A Suite of Modules on Coaching, Running Networks and Building Capacity* aimed to increase the range of tools available to school leaders to continually improve. In these relatively early days, the proposed form of coaching had a distinctly directive slant. However, the DfES was already optimistic about the impact of coaching, proposing that it "could have the power to transform teachers' professional learning" (p. 23). Coaching was described as a "three-part process" which focused on lesson observation. The process involved a pre-lesson discussion between the coach and coachee, an observation of the classroom practice of the coachee by the coach, and a post-lesson discussion to analyse what had been observed. While the document accepted that a coach was not a "universal expert", it suggested that this person should have "expertise in a particular area" that would be the focus of the coaching (p. 9). This point is further qualified when the document advocates that "coaching is often at its most powerful when the people involved teach different subjects" (p. 9). This is reinforced by the observation that the coach does not need to be "older, have more years of experience or hold a more senior management post" than the coachee (p. 23). Coaching in education, then, was an activity with classroom observation at its centre and professional learning as its aim. It involved two educational professionals, one with expertise in a particular area of practice, which was the focus of the coaching. The relationship was characterised as "confidential" and "based on trust" (ibid.). Importantly, there is recognition that ownership of the learning and the "desire to change and develop" should be within the coachee (p. 63).

Overall, the document can be interpreted as strongly supporting a specific interpretation of coaching and its use in an educational setting.

The DfES document was followed in 2005 by a *National Framework for Mentoring and Coaching* as a response to the growing interest (and confusion) in schools about the two approaches. The framework attempted to clarify the definitions of mentoring and coaching and identify how best to use both (Centre for the Use of Research and Evidence in Education (CUREE), 2005). This outstanding five-page framework continues to be a good reference document, although it has been largely ignored by the educational and coaching communities.

Without attempting to impose a uniform model for schools to adopt, the document listed ten principles which were designed to inform coaching and mentoring programmes in schools in order to "help increase the impact of continuing professional development on student learning" (ibid., p. 1). The similarities between coaching and mentoring are highlighted when they are both described as "learning conversations" and "thoughtful relationships" based on trust and focused on professional learning. The document advocated the establishment of learning agreements before coaching or mentoring with school colleagues to support improvement. It recommended that the learner (coachee or mentee) should take "increasing responsibility for their professional development" and set their own goals. The principles suggested that a learner should develop an understanding of the theories that underlie any new professional practice and recognise the professional learning that emerges from coaching and mentoring (for both parties). The creation of a context that "supports risk-taking and innovation" is encouraged.

After outlining the shared principles of coaching and mentoring, the document helpfully defined three terms to cover the broad range of professional conversations that can usefully take place in schools: mentoring, specialist coaching, and collaborative coaching. Mentoring is defined as a "structured, sustained process for supporting professional learners through significant career transitions" (p. 2) and further subdivided into three categories: Mentoring for Induction, Mentoring for Progression, and Mentoring for Challenge. In all cases, the assumption was that the mentor was a more senior professional with significant experience in the area of learning.

"Specialist coaching", which most closely resembles the practice promoted in the 2003 DfES document, was defined as "a structured, sustained process for enabling the development of a specific aspect of a professional learner's practice" (p. 2). Specialist coaching was deemed appropriate for improving practice, professional learning, and the development of a "culture of openness" (ibid.). One characteristic that distinguished specialist coaching from mentoring was the fact that the learner often chose their own coach.

The third category was "collaborative (co-) coaching", defined as a "sustained process between two or more professional learners to enable them to embed new knowledge and skills from specialist sources in day-to-day practice" (p. 2). This supported continuing professional development in schools by providing one-to-one support between peers to embed learning or expertise gleaned from elsewhere. What was unique about this relationship was its reciprocal nature—the peers are self-selecting and take turns in the role of coach.

The framework also defined the skills of each role, showing both the overlaps and differences. Although it was timely, helpful, and a sound basis for further work in this area, there is little evidence that it was widely adopted by local authorities, schools, or other government departments.

As coaching in education gained currency, the publication of *Leading Coaching in Schools* by the National College for School Leadership (Creasy & Paterson, 2005) further endorsed the use of coaching approaches within schools in the UK. A seminal publication that was well received in educational circles, the workbook built on the *National Framework for Mentoring and Coaching* with a definite focus on coaching. One of the workbook's propositions was that "high-quality coaching in schools supports professional development, leadership sustainability and school improvement" (p. 5), three topical areas of interest for the National College and the Department for Children, Schools, and Families. Adopting Suggett's definition of coaching as "unlocking potential in order to maximize performance—it's about bringing out the best in people", Creasy and Paterson (2005, p. 10) encouraged school leaders to start by developing themselves and then equip other members of staff with coaching skills.

Creasy and Paterson argued that coaching in education is driven by a "desire to make a difference to student learning". They identified five key skills which align with the non-directive coaching approaches which will be discussed in this book:

- establishing rapport and trust;
- listening for meaning;
- questioning for understanding;
- prompting action, reflection and learning;
- developing confidence and celebrating success (p. 14).

Preferring a non-directive approach, the workbook iterated that

as a general principle, it is not the role of the coach to provide answers or give advice. A core purpose of coaching is to support the development of the thinking and learning processes of the professional learner. (p. 17)

The authors addressed a possible area of confusion in the *National Framework* by explaining that "although specialist coaches may offer their own knowledge or experience, this occurs in response to direct requests as the learner seeks out specific information" (ibid.). The categories of coaching were expanded from two (specialist coaching and collaborative (co-) coaching) to seven. They now included "informal coaching conversations" (short conversations managed in a coaching style), "team coaching" (group sessions led by an external coach), "expert coaching" (training in coaching from an experienced external practitioner), "pupil coaching" (peer coaching between students), and "self-coaching" (using a coaching style for self-reflection).

Owing to a perceived lack of awareness about the *National Framework* (Lord, Atkinson, & Mitchell, 2008, p. vii), the Training and Development Agency for Schools (TDA) commissioned the National Foundation for Educational Research (NFER) to undertake further research on the evidence base for coaching and investigate how coaching and mentoring were being used in schools. While its intent was to update, validate, and increase awareness of the earlier framework, it seems to have had the opposite effect. Some might argue that the NFER research represents a retrograde step, since it adds to the confusion of terminology and undermines some of the clarity afforded by the initial work by CUREE. Their conclusion that "mentoring is defined as being concerned with 'growing an individual', both professionally and personally" and that it is "linked with professional and career development, and is somewhat characterised by an 'expert–novice' relationship" seems less clear than the conclusions of the earlier document. Equally, to define coaching as having "a narrower remit than mentoring" and relating to "specific areas of performance and job outcomes" further clouds the issue (p. 10).

With its focus on collaborative learning between practitioners in the classroom, Lesson Study is another National Strategy initiative that closely aligns with coaching. In the foreword to *Improving Practice and Progression through Lesson Study* (DfES, 2008), the Director of the National Strategies (primary), Pete Dudley, observed that "coaching is becoming increasingly well embedded within the work of LAs [local authorities] and schools, and through the work of National Strategies leading teachers and consultants". The document goes on to suggest that coaching is one of the ways in which teachers can share their learning and best practice.

The National College has also continued to support the use of coaching in schools and three of their professional development programmes for leaders (Leading from the Middle, Leadership Pathways, and National Professional Qualification for Headship) incorporate training on coaching. Participants in the three programmes can access coaches to support their learning (www.nationalcollege.org.uk).

Coaching was to have a significant role in an ambitious, large-scale, government-funded initiative to create a Masters-level programme for teachers called the Masters in Teaching and Learning (MTL). According to the TDA, "the school-based coach is integral to the Masters in Teaching and Learning (MTL) Programme" (p. 3). The role of the school-based coach is to "motivate and inspire, encourage on-going enquiry and reflection by the participant" (p. 3). While the TDA claims that "the principles of coaching within the MTL Programme are based on the National Framework for Mentoring and Coaching" (ibid.), the document suggests that the coach will also "identify needs relevant to the participant's school context, apply evidence and educational theory to real-life situations, in order to inform and consolidate their learning" (ibid.). Closer reading of the document suggests that the role envisaged for school-based coach combines elements of mentoring and "specialist coaching" as defined in the framework. While this initiative was quietly withdrawn in 2010 due to significant budget cuts across the public sector, the inclusion of coaching as a core element of the programme is indicative of the growing recognition that it has an important role to play in education.

## Instructional coaching and US approaches

There is growing acceptance in the USA that coaching is a necessary leadership skill for educators. In an edition dedicated to coaching, an influential USA magazine, *Educational Leadership*, featured articles from leading North American writers which all supported the development of various coaching approaches (*Educational Leadership*, 2011). This edition highlights some of the key US views about coaching in education.

The most influential of these approaches is instructional coaching, which has gained credibility and popularity in large parts of North America. An instructional coach is an "on-site" professional developer or adviser who teaches educators how to implement specific teaching methods. While instructional coaches are collaborative, they also have a role in preparing teaching materials, modelling best practice, observing teachers, and providing feedback (Knight, 2004). At the heart of instructional coaching is the notion that the relationship between professionals is a key factor when attending to learning and development. The founder of this approach, Jim Knight, discusses this in more depth in Chapter Six.

Alongside instructional coaching, the USA has also pioneered the idea of literacy coaches who have been employed to improve educational attainment (Moxley & Taylor, 2006; Sturtevant, 2003). Literacy coaching can be seen as "a category of instructional coaching that focuses on literacy and related aspects of teaching and learning" (Toll, 2009, p. 57) and involves "master teachers who provide essential leadership for the school's entire literacy program" (Sturtevant, 2003, p.11). Importantly, the primary role of the literacy coach is to work with other teachers, not students. They take more of a leadership role, carrying "the responsibility to promote and enhance literacy instruction with the ultimate goal of improving student achievement" (Moxley & Taylor, 2006, p. 8).

More recently, "evocative coaching" has emerged as a strengths-based approach for use in schools (Tschannen-Moran & Tschannen-Moran, 2010). Evocative coaching focuses on simple but effective techniques for having professional conversations in educational organisations and is closely allied to the non-directive coaching approach promoted in this book.

## Shared interest in learning

Formal education and coaching both share a fundamental interest in learning. Indeed, probably the strongest philosophy behind coaching and mentoring is that everyone has some potential to learn and develop. Using Bresser and Wilson's definition of coaching as "empowering people by facilitating self-directed learning, personal growth and improved performance" (2010, p. 10), it is clear that a key focus of coaching is the "self-directed" or personalised nature of the learning opportunity. Gross-Cheliotes and Reilly identify an important role of coaching when they propose that "coaching conversations foster the deep reflection necessary to establish new thinking patterns" (2010, p. 4). Whitmore's definition of coaching is perhaps the most apposite for educators: he describes it as "unlocking a person's potential to maximise their own performance" (2002, p. 8). This resonates with educators, since many would describe this as one of their prime personal and professional drivers. When working in educational organisations, this statement often leads to a genuine sense of "connection".

## How is coaching different from mentoring?

It should be acknowledged that there is confusion between the terms "coaching" and "mentoring". This tension is evident in the literature (for a detailed discussion, see Garvey, Stokes, & Megginson, 2009) and it is especially prevalent within education. A number of factors contribute to the current situation.

### Origin of the terminology

It has been argued that it is possible to trace the origins of coaching conversations to classical times. At the source of the confusion is the fact that one of the first coaches to be mentioned in the literature (the goddess Pallas Athena in Homer's *Odyssey*) assumed the role of

"Mentor" in order to help the adventurous Telemachus (de Haan, 2008, p. 5). Furthermore, the term "coach" might have derived from the term for horse-drawn carriages (Cox, Bachkirova, & Clutterbuck, 2009, p. 2), suggesting that the practice was associated with the idea of conveying a person from one place to another. The notion of taking someone from Point A to Point B suggests a slightly directive approach.

## Association with sports coaching

While current forms of executive coaching and life coaching have emerged from sports coaching (Downey, 2003; Gallwey, 2001; Whitmore, 2002), this association could also be clouding the issue. The *Oxford English Dictionary* defines a coach as someone who "trains others for an athletic contest" (*OED* online) while the *Merriam–Webster Dictionary* gives a football coach as an example: "one who instructs players in the fundamentals of a competitive sport and directs team strategy <a football *coach*>" (Merriam–Webster online). Many students will have experienced sports coaching through their involvement in school, college, or university sports teams and might, therefore, associate coaching with a more directive approach.

## Prevalence of mentoring programmes

Mentoring programmes have been successfully integrated into educational organisations. Many schools, colleges, and universities had already implemented mentoring schemes and were successfully using mentoring to support staff and students before the increased interest in coaching in education. Within many schools, colleges, and universities in the UK, students already have learning mentors. Newly qualified teachers (NQTs) and recently appointed head teachers are allocated a mentor when they start at a school. Buddy schemes in primary and secondary schools also create mentoring opportunities for students. Colleges and universities often have mentoring schemes for staff and students (see Chapter Thirteen for a case study).

To further cloud issues, the term "mentor coaching" has emerged and is defined as a "facilitated, structured process whereby an experienced person introduces, assists, and supports a less experienced person (the protégé) in a personal and professional growth process" (Nolan 2007, p. 3). As can be seen above, it can be used to achieve very positive results. We firmly believe that both coaching and mentoring can and should make a contribution within education.

## Similar but different?

As noted above, the National Framework for Mentoring and Coaching attempted to distinguish between the two approaches. There is a growing consensus that "coaching is not about telling, it is about asking and focusing. That is what separates mentoring from coaching" (Allison & Harbour, 2009, p. 2). The other significant difference often cited is the power relationship within the pairings. Coaching is often defined as "non-heirarchical and does not depend on any expert/subject specific knowledge" (ibid.). Passmore contrasts coaching and mentoring in the following areas: level of formality, length of contract, focus, level of sector knowledge, and training (2010, p. 5) (Table 1.1).

*Table 1.1.*   Contrasting coaching and mentoring (adapted from Passmore, 2010, p. 5).

|  | Coaching | Mentoring |
|---|---|---|
| *Level of formality* | *More formal*: contract or ground rules set, often involving the coachee's line manager | *Less formal*: agreement, most typically between two parties |
| *Length of engagement* | *Shorter term*: typically between 4 and 12 meetings agreed over 2 to 12 months | *Longer term*: typically, unspecified number of meetings with relationships often running over 3 to 5 years |
| *Focus* | *Focused on performance*: typically, a greater focus on short-term skills and job performance | *Focused on career development*: typically, a concern with longer-term career issues, obtaining the right experience |
| *Level of sector knowledge* | *More generalist*: typically, coaches have limited sector knowledge | *More sector knowledge*: typically, mentors have knowledge of organisation or business sector |

*(continued)*

*Table 1.1.   (continued).*

|  | Coaching | Mentoring |
|---|---|---|
| *Training* | *More relationship training*: typically, coaches have training in coaching-related skills | *More management training*: typically, mentors have a background in senior management |
| *Focus* | *Dual focus*: more typically a dual focus on the needs of the individual and the needs of the organisation | *Single focus*: more typically a single focus on the needs of the individual |

At the same time, many of the skills are similar. Coaches and mentors need to be good listeners. They need to ask powerful questions. Often, both will encourage their clients to pursue their ambitions and aspirations.

Rather than getting trapped in the debate over terminology, perhaps it would be more helpful to consider coaching and mentoring along a spectrum (Figure 1.1).

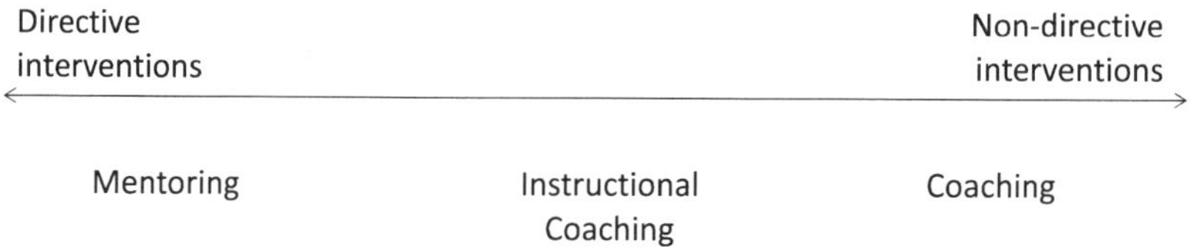

| Directive interventions | | Non-directive interventions |
|---|---|---|
| ← | | → |
| Mentoring | Instructional Coaching | Coaching |

*Figure 1.1.*   Coaching–mentoring continuum.

## *Purpose and intent*

Depending on the situation and the desired outcome, a more or less directive approach might be beneficial. For example, where the learner displays low levels of motivation to make behavioural changes, a more directive approach could be more helpful. Equally, in situations where a significant amount of information is needed for a new team member in a short period of time, an organisation might find that a more directive approach is most appropriate. On the other hand, in situations when the intention is to build self-esteem, independence, or self-confidence, a non-directive approach is certainly more likely to yield positive results.

Instructional coaching helpfully combines the non-directive elements of a collaborative way of working with some clearly directive elements. To ensure good outcomes for both parties (and, if relevant, their organisation), a negotiated agreement about the nature of the relationship should precede the learning conversations. Fundamentally, decisions about whether an interaction should be more or less directive should be driven by assessing the best interests of the recipient (coachee or mentee).

## Definition of educational coaching

For the purposes of this book, we will use the following definition of educational coaching: a one-to-one conversation focused on the enhancement of learning and development through increasing self-awareness and a sense of personal responsibility, where the coach facilitates the self-directed learning of the coachee through questioning, active listening, and appropriate challenge in a supportive and encouraging climate.

### One-to-one

While some suggest that "group coaching" is possible, we hold that coaching is most effective as a two-way conversation. Many of the benefits associated with coaching result from the confidential, supportive, and encouraging context and trusting relationship between two people. Once there are more than two people in a coaching relationship, group dynamics add a level of complexity that can impinge of the quality of trust and confidentiality. This is not to say that coaching approaches cannot also be used in group situations, in meetings and in the classroom. However, we believe that coaching is most effective in a one-to-one situation.

### Enhancement of learning and development through increasing self-awareness and a sense of personal responsibility

Coaching in education focuses on enhancing learning and development. This is done through increasing the self-awareness of the coachee, focusing primarily on strengths and existing resources. The sense of personal responsibility can emerge from the non-directive approach of the coach or a recognition that the coachee is best placed to effect the changes that they would like to see.

### Self-directed learning

We consider every coaching session to be a learning opportunity, primarily for the coachee (who may be seen as the primary learner), but also for the coach (secondary learner). Using a facilitative approach, the coach creates the context in which the coachee directs his or her own learning experience.

### Questioning, active listening, and appropriate challenge in a supportive and encouraging climate

As we will discuss in later chapters, we also believe that the activities of questioning, listening, and challenging should be carried out in a positive and encouraging climate. The coaching sessions should feel supportive and motivational. This approach models ways of relating that would be helpful in a broad range of educational and learning contexts.

Educational coaching, as described in this book, sits very comfortably at the non-directive end of the spectrum discussed above. We believe that educational coaching supports the development of responsibility, confidence, and self-esteem in learners through its non-directive approach. These learning conversations encourage and require the learner to find solutions and opportunities for themselves.

## The evidence

Although coaching in education is a relatively young field, there is a growing evidence base to support this area of work. Our interest in educational coaching stems from the belief that it can, in a number of different ways, positively affect learning experiences for both the "teacher" and the "student" in educational settings.

Coaching has been shown to have a positive impact on instructional practice in the classroom in an in-depth US study (Brown, Reumann-Moore, Hugh, Christman, & Riffer, 2008). Ross (1992) and

Shidler (2009) have demonstrated a clear link between the coaching of teachers and the achievement of their students. This evidence confirms a seemingly logical conclusion: that if coaching can have a beneficial impact on teachers, there would be a subsequent positive effect for the learning experiences of students.

It has been shown that the coaching of teachers can increase levels of student engagement (Brown, Reumann-Moore, Hugh, Christman, & Riffer, 2008). We also know that the preconceived expectations of teachers about their students can virtually predict performance levels (Rosenthal & Jacobson, 1968). Coaching can play an important role in supporting teachers to reflect on their practice in the classroom and encourage the development of professional learning relationships between educators (Brown, Reumann-Moore, Hugh, Christman, & Riffer 2008).

Evers, Brouwers, and Tomic (2006) have shown that executive coaching can lead to higher expectations about outcomes and self-efficacy. These findings are endorsed by Green, Oades, and Grant (2006), who demonstrated that life coaching increased goal attainment, well-being, and hope. A further study confirmed that personal coaching for students led to "significant increases in levels of cognitive hardiness and hope" (Green, Grant, & Rynsaardt, 2007). These results were supported by Spence and Grant (2007), who found that professional coaching for students increased goal commitment, goal attainment, and environmental mastery. In a significant regional study in the UK, Passmore and Brown (2009) found exam performance increased for sixteen-year-old students in poorly performing schools. More recent studies in the UK found that training secondary school students to become coaches had a positive impact on attitudes to learning (see Chapters Four and Eleven). Furthermore, Madden, Green, and Grant (2011) found that the use of solution focused coaching supported primary aged children in identifying their own strengths and resources. By visualising a positive future, children improved their engagement in learning as well as their sense of hope and improved wellbeing.

## Coaching in education: next steps

As early as 2005, it was recognised that coaching in education was important in the "quest to ensure that there are sufficient future leaders in the system to secure succession" (Creasy & Paterson, 2005) and that "learning to be a coach or mentor is one of the most effective ways of enabling teachers and leaders to become good and excellent practitioners" (CUREE, 2005). As we have shown above, there is also a growing body of evidence that points to significant benefits for students and educators.

Our experience of working in schools, colleges, and universities has shown us the potential impact of coaching on the way in which educators teach and students learn. Throughout this book, there are opportunities for self-reflection, suggestions for activities to enhance your coaching skills, and proposals for effective ways of implementing coaching within your educational organisation.

We will show how the creation of coaching cultures for learning can enhance the educational experience for everyone involved in this valuable enterprise. Educational institutions can encourage the development of lifelong learners who are self-aware and responsible. At a conference on coaching and positive psychology in education held on 2 July 2010, Sir John Whitmore challenged delegates to "teach less so that the students can learn more". What he was recommending was that, as educators, we also have a responsibility to encourage the development of the curiosity that comes naturally to all humans. There is something liberating about the ability to be comfortable with "not knowing". Since the majority of people in an educational organisation tend to be the "learners", it makes sense that "not knowing" is endorsed and celebrated. The anxiety about "not knowing", coupled with the pretence of "I know this already", can create a toxic mix that gets in the way of new learning opportunities. The first step is to lower our own defences, to become more comfortable with saying "I don't know", or "I don't really understand it myself". The infallible teacher or infallible educational leader only adds to the anxiety of other learners. When a student realises that we all learn, and that the process of learning involves the admission that we do not know everything, then it is easier for the student to take on the stance of learner.

The fact that you are reading this book is good news for your educational system! You are demonstrating that you are a learner who is interested in harnessing coaching to enhance the learning experience of everyone in your educational organisation. The audience for this book is both narrow and wide. It is narrow in the sense that this book is focused on educational organisations. It is wide in the sense that it is aimed at anyone who is passionate about education and believes in the principle that we are all lifelong learners.

In our experience of coaching within educational organisations, we have discovered that strong personal experiences of education (good or bad) are often motivating factors for some of our best educators. They are energised by the intention of making the learning experience as good as possible for others. They are passionate about removing barriers to learning and aspiration. We are convinced that coaching will support you to enhance the learning experience for everyone in your educational organisation while harnessing the energy and positive thinking of others to support you in this valuable endeavour.

## References

Allison, S., & Harbour, M. (2009). *The Coaching Toolkit: A Practical Guide for Your School.* London: Sage.

Bresser, F., & Wilson, C. (2010). What is coaching? In: J. Passmore (Ed.), *Excellence in Coaching: The Industry Guide* (pp. 9–26). London: Kogan Page.

Brown, D., Reumann-Moore, R., Hugh, R., Christman, J. B., & Riffer, M. (2008). *Links to Learning and Sustainability: Year Three Report of the Pennsylvania High School Coaching Initiative.* Philadelphia, PA: Research for Action.

Centre for the Use of Research and Evidence in Education (2005). *Mentoring and Coaching CPD Capacity Building Project (2004–2005): National Framework for Mentoring and Coaching.* London: CUREE.

Cox, E., Bachkirova, T., & Clutterbuck, D. (Eds.) (2010). *The Complete Handbook of Coaching.* London: Sage.

Creasy, J., & Paterson, F. (2005). *Leading Coaching in Schools.* London: National College for School Leadership.

de Haan, E. (2008). *Relational Coaching: Journeys towards Mastering One-to-one Learning.* Chichester: Wiley.

Dembkowski, S., Eldridge, F., & Hunter, I. (2006). *The Seven Steps of Effective Executive Coaching.* London: Thorogood.

Department for Children, Schools and Families (2008). *Improving Practice and Progression through Lesson Study: Handbook for Headteachers, Leading Teachers and Subject Leaders.* London: DCSF.

Department for Children, Schools and Families (2009). *Your Child, Your Schools, Our Future: Building a 21st Century Schools System.* London: DCSF.

Department for Education (2010). Retrieved 4 September from www2. ed.gov/about/what-we-do.html

Department for Education and Skills (2003). *Sustaining Improvement: A Suite of Modules on Coaching, Running Networks and Building Capacity.* London: DfES.

Dewey, J. (1916). *Democracy and Education: An Introduction to the Philosophy of Education.* New York: Macmillan.

Downey, M. (2003). *Effective Coaching: Lessons from the Coach's Coach* (3rd edn). Florence, KY: Cengage Learning.

*Educational Leadership* (2011). Volume *69*(2), October.

Evers, W. J. G., Brouwers, A., & Tomic, W. (2006). A quasi-experimental study on management: coaching effectiveness. *Consulting Psychology Journal: Practice and Research, 58*(3): 174–182.

Gallwey, W. T. (2001). *Inner Game of Work: Focus, Learning, Pleasure and Mobility in the Workplace.* New York: Random House.

Garvey, R., Stokes, P., & Megginson, D. (2009). *Coaching and Mentoring: Theory and Practice.* London: Sage.

Grant, A. M. (2007). Past, present and future: the evolution of professional coaching and coaching psychology. In: S. Palmer & A. Whybrow (Eds.), *Handbook of Coaching Psychology: A Handbook for Practitioners* (pp. 23–39). London: Routledge.

Green, L. S., Oades, L. G., & Grant, A. M. (2006). Cognitive–behavioral, solution-focused life coaching: enhancing goal striving, well-being, and hope. *Journal of Positive Psychology, 1*(3): 142–149.

Green, S., Grant, A.M., & Rynsaardt, J. (2007). Evidence-based life coaching for senior high school students: Building hardiness and hope. *International Coaching Psychology Review, 2*(1): 24–32.

Gross-Cheliotes, L., & Reilly, M. F. (2010). *Coaching Conversations: Transforming Your School One Conversation at a Time.* London: Sage.

Hawkins, P., & Smith, N. (2006). *Coaching, Mentoring and Organizational Consultancy: Supervision and Development.* Maidenhead: Open University Press.

Jeffreys, M. (1971). *Education: Its Nature and Purpose.* London: Unwin.

Knight, J. (2004). Instructional coaches make progress through partnership: intensive support can improve teaching. *Journal of Staff Development, 25*(2): 32–37.

Lord, P., Atkinson, M., & Mitchell, H. (2008). *Mentoring and Coaching for Professionals: A Study of the Research Evidence.* London: National Foundation for Educational Research.

Madden, W., Green, S., & Grant, A. M. (2011). A pilot study evaluating strengths-based coaching for primary school students: enhancing engagement and hope. *International Coaching Psychology Review*, 6(1): 71–83.

*Merriam–Webster Dictionary* online. http://www.merriam-webster.com/

Moxley, D. E., & Taylor, R. T. (2006). *Literacy Coaching: A Handbook for School Leaders.* Thousand Oaks, CA: Corwin.

Nolan, M. E. (2007). *Mentor Coaching and Leadership in Early Care and Education.* New York: Thomson.

Oxford English Dictionary online. www.oed.com/

Passmore, J. (Ed.) (2010). *Excellence in Coaching: The Industry Guide* (2nd edn). London: Kogan Page.

Passmore, J., & Brown, A. (2009). Coaching non-adult students for enhanced examination performance: a longitudinal study. *Coaching: An International Journal of Theory, Research and Practice*, 2(1): 54–64.

Peltier, B. (2010). *The Psychology of Executive Coaching: Theory and Application* (2nd edn). New York: Routledge.

Rosenthal, R., & Jacobson, L. (1968). *Pygmalion in the Classroom.* New York: Holt, Rinehart & Winston.

Ross, J. A. (1992). Teacher efficacy and the effect of coaching on student achievement. *Canadian Journal of Education*, 17(1): 51–65.

Shidler, L. (2009). The impact of time spent coaching for teacher efficacy on student achievement. *Early Childhood Education Journal*, 36(5): 453–460.

Spence, G. B., & Grant, A. M. (2007). Professional and peer life coaching and the enhancement of goal striving and well-being: An exploratory study. *The Journal of Positive Psychology*, 2(3): 185–194.

Sturtevant, E. G. (2003). *The Literacy Coach: A Key to Improving Teaching and Learning in Secondary Schools.* Washington, DC: Alliance for Excellent Education.

Toll, C. A. (2009). Literacy coaching. In: J. Knight (Ed.), *Coaching: Approaches and perspectives.* (pp. 56–69). Thousand Oaks, CA: Corwin.

Training and Development Agency for Schools (2009). *Masters in Teaching and Learning: Coaching Strategy.* London: TDA.

Tschannen-Moran, B., & Tschannen-Moran, M. (2010). *Evocative Coaching: Transforming Schools One Conversation at a Time.* San Francisco, CA: Jossey-Bass.

Whitmore, J. (2002). *Coaching for Performance: Growing People, Performance and Purpose.* (3rd edn). London: Nicholas Brealey.

# CHAPTER TWO

# Coaching and mentoring for educational leadership

*Christian van Nieuwerburgh*

## Introduction

Educational leadership is uniquely challenging and can be particularly rewarding. It combines leadership of people, learning, and complex organisations. Many in educational leadership positions have been attracted to the role by a desire to make a real difference to people's lives. Often, they have successful track records as outstanding educators, almost always with direct experience of teaching or lecturing in the classroom. This chapter considers how coaching and mentoring can support educational leaders and their organisations to flourish.

## Educational leadership

Leadership is a concept that has fascinated us as a human race throughout our history. In our attempts to define it, we have made reference to a broad range of models, variously alluding to historical figures, military heroes, dramatic characters, poets, philosophers, architects, and strategic planners. We have grappled with the nuanced differences between leadership and management, at times narrowed, and at other times broadened, the scope of leadership to include the very few at the top or the vast majority of people within an organisation. Recently, we have begun to wonder how leadership relates to "followership", and whether the leader should lead from the front, the middle, or the rear.

However, we do seem to have a shared understanding of what we mean by "leadership", and, more importantly, we are agreed that "the leader, through his or her behaviours, has the biggest impact on team climate" (Fitzsimmons & Guise, 2010, p. 233). Taking into account the powerful impact that leadership can have on organisations, it is appropriate to consider how coaching can support educational leaders in their roles. Educational leadership has been defined as

> a process of influence based on clear values and beliefs and leading to a 'vision' for the school. The vision is articulated by leaders who seek to gain the commitment of staff and stakeholders to the ideal of a better future for the school, its students and stakeholders. (Bush, 2011, p. 198)

It is my belief that educational leaders are "lead learners" within their organisations. To be an authentic, engaged educational leader is to role model a positive approach to learning, embracing the opportunity to be a lead learner. Equally, I would argue that, despite the many books that continue to flood the market, there is no "blueprint" for leadership success and few simple answers to the complex notion of leadership. Rather, every organisation and every context requires its own leadership approach. And it is precisely the lack of a "one-size-fits-all" leadership solution that creates the need for one-to-one personalised support in the form of coaching.

## Leadership coaching

Leadership coaching has been shown to have real potential in the private and public sectors by "improving leadership in those with high potential, facilitating transitions to larger jobs, on-boarding those new to the organization, and developing a selected group of individuals with specific needs" (Furnham, 2010, p. 127). It is now accepted that coaching can support leaders in commercial organisations in a number of ways:

- helping leaders to transfer theoretical learning to workplace practice;
- enhancing skills and developing new habits;
- developing greater self awareness;
- enhancing motivation;
- strengthening personal confidence and self-regard;
- building resilience and supporting well-being (Passmore, 2010).

In this chapter, we propose that coaching can support educational leaders in the same ways. Furthermore, we propose that there are additional benefits for educational organisations.

## Coaching for educational leadership

In the educational arena, coaching and mentoring are already being used to support new and aspiring head teachers and college principals. As discussed above, there is certainly a role for coaching to support educational leaders to make the transition between one organisation and other. Many newly appointed head teachers already benefit from the support and advice of a mentor (often another head teacher) during their first year in post. In the UK, National College leadership programmes (including *Leading from the Middle* and *National Professional Qualification for Headship*) offer coaching support alongside a range of other blended learning opportunities.

In addition to these traditional approaches, this chapter will consider further applications for coaching which can enhance leadership effectiveness, support succession planning, and reconnect to moral purpose. We will conclude by suggesting practical ways of developing coaching skills in educational organisations and consider the use of a coaching model to support educational leaders.

## Skills of coaching and educational

There is a natural synergy between educational leadership and effective coaching. Creasy and Paterson have suggested that coaching in education is driven by "a desire to make a difference to student learning" (2005). This is, without a doubt, a key motivator for school and college leaders. Furthermore, it is true to say that coaching and education have a shared focus on learning for personal and professional development.

Through our own coaching practice and experience of teaching coaching skills to others, we have identified the following skill set as being important for effective coaching:

---

**Key skills and abilities for coaches**

- showing accurate empathy and accurate listening;
- relating well to others;
- being able to put things into perspective for one's self and others;
- focusing on positives and finding strengths in one's self and others;
- remaining objective and fair, even when under pressure;
- maintaining an open-minded and non-judgemental stance;
- being able to challenge others to achieve more of their potential;
- being able to give appropriate feedback to support development.

---

In fact, Bloom, Castagna, Moir, and Warren (2005) describe "relationship building", "listening, observing and questioning", and "giving feedback" as the "foundational" skills of coaching (p. 25). These foundational skills are further reinforced by the ideal "attitude" of a coach:

- empathy, respect, warmth and authenticity in relation to the coachee;
- tolerance and openness to different values and opinions;
- an appropriate balance between detachment and involvement;
- an encouraging and gentle approach towards the coachee;
- readiness to let the other person take initiative and responsibility;
- an attitude of service towards their coachees, helping them to (learn how to) progress themselves;
- an inclination to give as little advice as possible (even if that is requested), based on the conviction that giving advice is often an insult to the other person, who has already spent a long time thinking about the issue and can give the best advice himself or herself;
- a confrontational approach only if the coachee can take it and benefit from it, otherwise a preference for supportive interventions
- humour and an ability to put things into perspective. (De Haan, 2008, p. 161)

The skills and attitude represented above should be familiar to educational leaders. It is our belief that these skills and attitude are equally as necessary for educational leaders as they are for coaches. Indeed, many successful educational leaders demonstrate these skills on a daily basis. One way in which coaching can be experienced in educational organisations is through the leadership style of its senior leaders. According to the National College for School Leadership, "leaders should model the dialogue and personal approaches that create a culture of high-quality coaching interaction across the school" (Creasy & Paterson, 2005, p. 5). Coaching cultures for learning are discussed later (in Chapter Nine), but it is worth noting that school and college leaders who embrace a "coaching style" of leadership can have an immediate positive impact across their organisations.

As we consider the synergy between education and coaching, a parallel emerges between a "coaching style" and emotionally intelligent leadership. Emotional intelligence (EI or EQ) is a concept that has been studied over the last two decades (Bar-On & Parker, 2000; Bar-On, Maree, & Elias, 2007; Goleman, 1995, 1998). Recent research has confirmed a supposed link between levels of emotional intelligence and leadership ability (Bar-On, 2003; Bharwaney, Bar-On, & MacKinlay, 2007). There are striking similarities between the skills and attitude of a coach (discussed above) and the characteristics of emotionally intelligent leaders:

Emotionally intelligent leaders often display the following characteristics:

- They cope proactively with life's demands and pressures without caving in.
- They build and leverage cooperative, effective and rewarding relationships with others.
- They are able to set and achieve personal and professional goals in a manner that is compatible with what is best for them and others.
- They seek first to understand, and then to be understood.
- They are sufficiently assertive and act with authority in making difficult and courageous decisions when the need arises.
- They are typically positive and lead by example.
- They are realistically optimistic about maximising their potential and able to get the most out of others. (Perks & Bar-On, 2010, p. 56)

Coaching has been identified as an ideal way of developing emotionally intelligent leadership (Fitzsimmons & Guise, 2010). Initially, coaches can support leaders to learn and use six leadership styles (Goleman, 2000):

- directive or coercive style.
  - being clear about tasks that need to be completed and expecting compliance;
- visionary or authoritative style;
  - communicating the "big picture" and helping others to share in the organisational vision;
- affiliative style;
  - valuing the contributions of others and taking into account the emotional needs of team members;
- democratic or participative style;
  - seeking the views of others, building a vision together and sharing responsibility with team members;
- pacesetting style;
  - leading by example, getting things done quickly and efficiently;
- coaching style;
  - learning about the aspirations of individual team members and supporting each to fulfil more of their potential. (Fitzsimmons & Guise, 2010)

Goleman highlights the strengths and weaknesses of each approach, recommending that leaders learn when and how to use each of the styles to best effect. According to Fitzsimmons and Guise, coaches can support this process by helping leaders to "diagnose the demands of the situation", "select the right response to meet those demands", and "keep an open mind and watch out for changes in the situation that require a different approach" (Fitzsimmons & Guise, 2010, p. 232). More generally, coaching creates a positive and relatively safe environment for educational leaders to explore their leadership approach and the impact that this might be having on their peers, staff, students, and members of the community.

## Educational leaders as coaches

An important part of emotionally intelligent leadership is the ability to support the development of others ("coaching style"). Educational leaders have an important role as coach or mentor for aspiring leaders in their organisations. We have already discussed in some detail the "directive to non-directive spectrum" of coaching in Chapter One.

A key skill of educational leaders is the ability to identify the most appropriate, supportive intervention when opportunities arise. Knowing when to support someone through non-directive coaching as opposed to a more directive approach is an important skill for anyone in a leadership position. In an educational context, mentoring (which we have suggested is closer to the directive end of the spectrum) is the more common form of one–one support currently available for aspiring leaders. Bloom, Castagna, Moir, and Warren (2005, p. 28) assert that "it is frequently necessary for coaches to withhold their personal expertise so their coachees can develop individual, internal capacity". Some educational leaders find it difficult to withhold advice, often with the best intentions. It might seem counter-intuitive to withhold "personal expertise" when a colleague is seemingly in need of an answer. In many cases, educational leaders recognise that their personal expertise is the reason that they have been promoted to a leadership position, so there is an understandable desire to share this. Another often mentioned reason for providing an "answer" is the perceived lack of time within educational organisations. Faced with little time and "initiative overload" (Abrahamson, 2004), educational leaders often find that it is quickest to provide an immediate solution.

A key development area for some educational leaders is the ability to question any tendency to automatically take the stance of a mentor. A helpful question to ask at this point is: "What type of support will increase the likelihood of a positive and sustainable outcome in this situation for this individual?" It is important to determine which type of intervention (directive or non-directive) would be most helpful. Every situation is different and will require individual consideration by an emotionally intelligent leader. In the spirit of being person-centred, the primary driver should be the best, longer term interest of the coachee. Based on my experience of working with coaches, educational leaders, and clients, I would like to share the following examples, with reference to helpful interventions in Table 2.1 and some examples of less helpful interventions in Table 2.2.

*Table 2.1.*   Helpful interventions.

| Situation | Intention (of educational leader) | Intervention (of educational leader) | Ideal outcome (for team member) |
|---|---|---|---|
| Team member frequently comes to the leader with questions, concerns and problems | To enhance self-confidence and self-esteem | Non-directive: (What do you think? What are you going to do?) | "I am capable and resourceful, able to complete tasks and handle challenges on my own." |
| Team member is not proactive, waiting until "told" to undertake certain tasks | To increase awareness of intrinsic motivation | Non-directive: (What interests you? What would you like to do?) | "The leader seems interested in me. I find that being an active member of the team is rewarding." |
| Team member is easily discouraged and demoralised | To build resilience | Non-directive: (What did you do well that you would want to repeat? What will you do differently next time?) | "The leader thinks that I will be able to get it right. I'll try again. I may be able to "bounce back" from temporary setbacks." |
| Team member needs information for imminent meeting | To provide relevant data | Directive: (What information do you need? Here it is.) | "I have the information I need to handle this meeting well." |
| Team member has overcommitted and needs "a break" | To minimise causes of stress | Directive: (I'll take care of this issue.) | "I have one thing less to worry about." |
| Team member needs a solution to an unexpected problem immediately | To provide a quick solution | Directive: (What about trying . . .?) | "There's someone there in case of an emergency." |

*Table 2.2.* Unhelpful interventions.

| Situation | Intention | Intervention | Unwanted outcome |
|---|---|---|---|
| Team member frequently comes to the leader with questions, concerns, and problems | To answer questions, reassure, and solve problems | Directive: (Why don't you try this? I think it will work.) | "I am not capable of dealing with these issues on my own. I will be back when this issue arises again." |
| Team member is not proactive, waiting until "told" to undertake certain tasks | To achieve outcomes | Directive: (I would like you to do . . .) | "It's just a job. If I keep my head down, there will be less to do." |
| Team member is easily discouraged and demoralised | To comfort | Directive: (Don't worry about it. It's not a big deal. I'll ask someone else to do it next time.) | "I'm no good at that. I was right when I thought that I wouldn't be able to do it." |
| Team member needs information for imminent meeting | To encourage independence | Non-directive: (Where could you get this information? What might you do differently before the next meeting?) | "I do not get the support I need to do my job effectively. I won't go to this person for advice any more." |
| Team member has overcommitted and needs "a break" | To build resilience | Non-directive: (What are you going to do? Who could help you with this situation?) | "I have too much on my mind. I don't know how I will cope." |
| Team member needs a solution to an unexpected problem immediately | To build self-confidence | Non-directive: (What possible solutions are there?) | "My leader takes no responsibility. I am on my own." |

## Coaching for succession planning

Over the past decade, there has been growing concern in the UK about a perceived shortage of future educational leaders, especially in primary schools. A recent report commissioned by the National Association of Head Teachers raises a serious concern about the "appointment of new head teachers, and especially within parts of the primary school sector, and the whole of the special school sector". The authors find that

> close on a third of primary schools and around four out of ten special schools cannot make an appointment [of a head teacher] when advertising a vacancy some six years after the introduction of a mandatory qualification [the National Professional Qualification for Headship]. (Howson & Sprigade, 2010, p. 136)

In 2005, an NCSL publication made an explicit link between coaching and leadership development, declaring that coaching can have an important role to play in the "quest to ensure that there are sufficient future leaders in the system to secure succession" (Creasy & Paterson, 2005). I often ask groups of senior teachers on training programmes how many of them are planning to go on to headship. It is common that less than 10% of participants respond positively! Obviously, there will be many reasons for the perceived shortage in aspiring school leaders who are willing to step up to the challenges of headship.

---

*What's stopping teachers from aspiring to headship?*

Perception of headship as stressful and unrewarding.

Perception of the work/life imbalance for many head teachers (long hours culture).

The relatively small salary differentials (in primary schools) between head teachers and deputy or assistant head teachers.

A reluctance to become distant from the classroom.

The lack of opportunity to openly discuss aspirations and career progression.

Coaching can make an immediate contribution in this area. The safe, confidential nature of coaching allows aspiring leaders to increase awareness about their own personal and professional goals. The sessions provide a non-judgemental space in which potential future leaders can explore their thoughts, anxieties, and dreams about educational leadership. Coachees report that it is helpful to explore their ideas with an objective and non-evaluative other. Often, just talking about the possibility of more senior leadership roles can create a positive momentum towards further learning and development opportunities. In these situations, coaching and mentoring are complementary approaches, and I believe that both are needed for leadership development in the education sector. A non-directive coach without a vested interest in the future plans of a potential future leader is an ideal opportunity for a coachee to genuinely explore their options, consider a balanced view of headship, reconnect with their "moral compass" and make clear and thoughtful decisions about their future.

## Coaching across the system

Now, more than ever, there is a pressing need for educational leaders to work together to develop coaching resources across the system. There is obviously a role here for leaders in the educational system to support the growth and development of future leadership. While conceding that it is not necessary for a coach to have been a secondary school head teacher in order to coach another secondary school head teacher, Bloom, Castagna, Moir, and Warren (2005) insist that the coach should "have a strong grasp of the issues faced by high school leaders and a vision for a quality secondary education" (ibid., p. 111). There are distinct advantages to head teachers and college principals providing coaching support to one another. As peers, they are likely to be able to quickly build rapport with each other and empathise more appropriately than an external, non-educationalist coach. As a result, the coaching conversations might be able to delve more deeply into topics rather than spending time on superficial issues. Bloom, Castagna, Moir, and Warren (2005) concur when they propose that

the role of a school leadership coach is to try always to move coaching conversations and interventions beyond the immediate issues to those underlying opportunities for system improvement that are likely to have the greatest positive impact on students. (p. 109)

Robertson (2008) emphasises the potential mutuality of leader-to-leader support when she defines coaching as

a special, sometimes reciprocal, relationship between (at least) two people who work together to set professional goals *and* achieve them. The term depicts a learning relationship, where participants are open to new learning, engage together as professionals equally committed to facilitating each other's leadership learning development and well-being (both cognitive and affective), and gain a greater understanding of professionalism and the work of professionals. (p. 4)

To suggest that coaching is about the "development of the recognised processes of appraisal and performance management" (Taylor, 2007) is no longer helpful. There is a growing consensus within the educational community that coaching can have a broad and significant impact on educational leadership.

If we believe that a coaching style for leadership, coaching support for staff in schools, and peer coaching and mentoring opportunities for educational leaders can have a significant impact on learning, what needs to happen for us to reap the potential rewards?

## Building coaching skills in educational organisations

In a 2005 report, the Centre for the Use of Research and Evidence in Education recognised that it was "widely accepted that the opportunity to learn through becoming a mentor or coach has a dramatic and positive effect on the skills of the mentor or coach". The report concludes that "learning to be a coach or mentor is one of the most effective ways of enabling teachers or leaders to *become* good and excellent practitioners" (CUREE, 2005, p. 7). This means that training educational staff in coaching skills can have multiple benefits: the creation of a coaching resource for staff and students within the organisation; the possibility of participating in local, regional, or national coaching initiatives supporting other educational professionals; more effective and better supported educational leaders and better educational practitioners.

*Skills development*

It is important that the need for coaching skills is identified by staff and not imposed by leaders in educational organisations. In my view, the best way of convincing others of the benefits is for them to experience coaching for themselves. If this is not possible, a brief, open, no-obligation, awareness-raising session on coaching might be helpful. Ultimately, the organisation must *want* to develop a coaching culture. (Coaching cultures for learning are explored further in Chapter Nine.)

Once there has been agreement about the need to develop coaching-related skills, much of the necessary professional development can be delivered in-house, especially in secondary schools and further education colleges. Otherwise, many professional development organisations now offer short courses on coaching and a number of universities have coaching programmes ranging from postgraduate certificates to Masters level qualifications.

In many ways, the joint activity of developing the necessary skills within organisations, using existing knowledge and expertise, might be the most fruitful and productive way of embracing a coaching culture. Educational organisations interested in pursuing coaching approaches will need to consider their preferred ways of developing the following skills:

- active listening;
- asking powerful questions;
- emotional intelligence;
- giving and receiving feedback;
- providing helpful challenge.

As we have already implied, many of these skills already exist within the educational workforce, perhaps more than in other professions. An appreciative approach that builds on these existing skills is most likely to be well received. The process itself and opportunities for peer coaching will have the added benefit of enhancing another necessary attribute: greater self-awareness. As Sergiovanni and Starratt suggest, "educational leadership requires leaders to make their values, beliefs, and interests transparent to others—to identify and articulate their educational platforms" (2002, p. 30). Furthermore, success in introducing coaching skills and a coaching approach will strengthen the self-confidence of individuals and the organisation.

## *Johari's Window on to educational leadership*

One particularly helpful coaching model is an adapted version of Johari's Window (Luft & Ingham, 1955) (Figure 2.1). Called the "Johari's Window on to educational leadership", the model has four quadrants, each representing a potenial area of learning. The focal point for the purposes of coaching is the upper left hand quadrant, here called the "educational persona". In the lower left, there is the "hidden self" quadrant. The upper right quadrant is the "learning and development" quadrant. The lower right quadrant, which we have playfully dubbed the "Rumsfeld corner" represents the "unknown". In the background is a circle that represents the educational work context of the coachee.

When used for educational leadership coaching, the following steps can be taken, although these can be adapted by the coach.

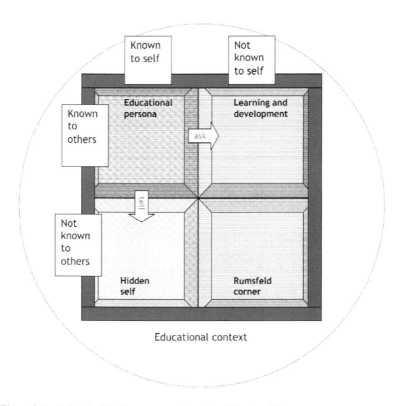

*Figure 2.1.* Johari's Window on to educational leadership.

1. Introduce the model.
   There are four quadrants and an "educational context" field.

*Top left:* Educational persona
This is the one that will be of most interest. The purpose of this coaching discussion is to enlarge this quadrant. This quadrant represents "what is generally known" about the coachee in their educational role (i.e., Information that is "known to self" and "known to others").

*Bottom left:* Hidden self
This quadrant contains information that we have not disclosed in our professional role. This could include personal experiences, strong emotional drivers, religious or spiritual beliefs, and world views. The key question when addressing this quadrant is whether sharing some of this information will enhance the coachee's educational persona. By definition, this quadrant includes information that is "not known to others" but "known to self".

*Top right:* Learning and development
This quadrant contains information that we do not yet "know". What is discussed in this quadrant is what others have said to or about the coachee (i.e., information that is "known to others" but "not known to self"). This can be confusing to explain, but will become clearer during the discussion.

*Bottom right:* Rumsfeld corner
I call this the Rumsfeld corner, based on an attempted explanation by the former US defence secretary, Donald Rumsfeld, during a press briefing in 2003, of the complexity of leadership:

> Reports that say that something hasn't happened are always interesting to me, because as we know, there are known knowns; there are things we know we know. We also know there are known unknowns; that is to say we know there are some things we do not know. But there are also unknown unknowns—the ones we don't know we don't know.

To be fair to Rumsfeld, this is a relatively mysterious quadrant that contains information that is not known by the coachee, the coach, or anyone else in the coachee's educational context. Through coaching, any new information that emerges that surprises the coachee and is unknown to anyone else would inhabit this quadrant. For example, if a coachee discovers, through journal writing for the purposes of the coaching, that they have a natural skill and tendency towards creative writing, this would be considered to be growing the educational persona through discovering unknown potential.

*Educational context*
Underlying the Johari window is the educational context in which the coachee operates. The contextual circle exists to acknowledge the impact that the context might have on the educational persona of the coachee. Within this circle are represented all the stakeholders of the educational organisation: learners, governors, parents, central and local government (if appropriate). An educational professional does not exist in a vacuum, and it is useful to regularly refer to the educational context during the coaching conversation.

2. Start the coaching session by considering the "educational persona" quadrant. This is an opportunity for the coach and the coachee to build rapport and get a shared understanding of the "current reality". The questioning should focus on how the coachee is perceived within their educational setting (e.g., "If I were to visit your school/college and talk to a few of the staff, asking them to tell me about you, what do you think they would say about you?"). As the coachee shares their thoughts, it is helpful if they could also bullet-point these and write them into the "educational persona" quadrant. The coach should take an appreciative stance, recognising strengths and encouraging the coachee to celebrate achievements. Once the "educational persona" quadrant has been completed and both the coachee and coach have a shared understanding of the coachee's educational persona (as it is perceived within the coachee's organisation), the coach can ask how the coachee would *like* to be perceived (in an ideal world) in their professional role. The coach should recognise which elements are already in place and the gap between the "current reality" and the aspiration could inform some of the coachee's goals.

During this discussion, it is important to reflect on the educational context circle, seeing how that has shaped (to some extent) the educational persona of the coachee. Equally, once the coachee has described their ideal persona, it might be helpful to ask the coachee how aligned that is with the ideal that might be described by those representing the educational context. This alignment is crucial for sustained educational leadership success.

3. Next, time is spent talking about the "hidden self" in relation to the coachee's stated goals. The reason for delving into this quadrant is to consider whether sharing some of the coachee's moral purpose, integrity, and beliefs would enhance their educational persona and support the coachee to achieve their goal. In other words, would being more explicit about their deeply held beliefs support the coachee in their educational role? Another purpose of this discussion is to reconnect the coachee to their motivation and talk about underlying beliefs about learning and education. These can be powerful drivers for any necessary change. Once again, invite the coachee to bullet-point their thoughts in the quadrant. The final stage is to decide which of those bullet points they would like to transfer into the "educational persona" quadrant. Obviously, the coach should handle this information sensitively, as there are often good reasons why coachees have chosen to keep certain information "hidden". In the model, the "tell" arrow suggests that the most appropriate way of adding elements of the "hidden self" into the "educational persona" is to disclose that information in some way. This is now discussed. How can the coachee expand the "educational persona" by introducing some elements of the "hidden self"? It is appropriate at this point to support the coachee to consider ways of doing this. Once a number of options have been considered and evaluated, the coach seeks commitment to an achievable number of actions that will be reviewed at a future coaching session.

4. The final quadrant for in-depth discussion is "learning and development". This discussion centres on increasing self-awareness through feedback from others. Starting this part of the coaching conversation with the question "What do others know about you that you do not know" leads to the obvious and awkward answer, "I don't know", which is precisely the point of the exercise. What is being sought in this section is a consideration of the views of others through the lens of the coachee. In other words, what have people in the circular educational context said about the coachee that has not been incorporated into the educational persona? For some reason, information has been rejected and the intention is to reconsider whether learning could emerge. For example, a coachee might say, "A few people have mentioned that I can be intimidating but I guess they don't know me that well." This is worth exploring during the coaching session. What

situations were being discussed? What was the context for those observations? Equally, there will be cases where the feedback is seemingly positive: "People often say that I am very professional and calm under pressure. What they don't know is that I'm all over the place inside. I must be good at hiding how I really feel." Again, what can be learnt from these comments? What examples are there of the coachee being "professional and calm under pressure"? An important element of the discussion around this quadrant is about getting more information so that it increases the coachee's awareness of themselves. In essence, the reason some of this information is not in the educational persona is because the *coachee* has rejected it. However, before incorporating this information, it is again useful for the coachee to consider some practical actions to solicit feedback. Often, it is simply a case of the coachee asking colleagues "How do you think that went?" or "How did I come across at that meeting?" In other cases, it might be helpful for a coachee to keep a journal, recording informal feedback regularly for discussion at future coaching sessions. Depending on the nature of the engagement between the coach and the coachee, it could also be appropriate for the educational leader to ask the coach to observe them in their professional role. By "shadowing" the educational leader, the coach would be providing valuable support in collecting data to inform future discussions relating to the "learning and development" arena.

5. It might be worth briefly asking the coachee whether any new insights have emerged within the "Rumsfeld corner". New information can sometimes be uncovered during coaching sessions or in between sessions. The fourth quadrant is not a necessary part of the coaching process; rather, it acknowledges that everyone has potential which may be discovered "accidentally".

6. The final stage of the coaching conversation returns to the "educational persona" quadrant. The coach might recap (positively) the traits of the educational leader as described within the quadrant and gain commitment for the agreed actions. A review of the process (with feedback for the coach) would be useful here.

In practice, I have found Johari's Window on to educational leadership to be an effective and appropriate tool for coaching head teachers and aspiring leaders. The "hidden self" quadrant often allows for discussion about moral purpose, integrity, and strongly held beliefs about children, young people, or learners. It allows discussion of motivation and "meaning", which may have become obscured over time. Reconnection with these strongly motivational beliefs can provide the renewed energy and enthusiasm that is necessary for sustainable change. The process leads to increased self-awareness while also encouraging practical actions for the coachee to take. With an enhanced appreciation of how the educational context (or expectations) has an impact on their own educational persona, school and college leaders become more conscious of how they are perceived in their workplace.

## Conclusion

Coaching can support educational leaders to continue to perform effectively and with commitment, and it is also a useful tool for bringing out the best in educational staff and students; it can also leverage organisational change within schools and colleges and systemic change across the wider educational arena. A leading international educational reformer, Michael Fullan, shares a "glimpse of the new moral imperative" of educational leadership: to lead "deep cultural change that mobilises the passion and commitment of teachers, parents, and others to improve the learning of all students, including closing the achievement gap" (2003, p. 41). Ultimately, it is helpful to remind ourselves that "people change organisations. The starting point is not system change, or change in those around us, but taking action ourselves" (Fullan, 1992, p. 61).

## References

Abrahamson, E. (2004). *Change without Pain: How Managers Can Overcome Initiative Overload, Organizational Chaos, and Employee Burnout*. Boston, MA: Harvard Business School.

Bar-On, R. (2003). The impact of EI on leadership and organizational productivity: how to make the case in 45 minutes. A presentation delivered to The Consortium for Research on Emotional Intelligence in Organizations. Boston, MA: 30 October 2003.

Bar-On, R., & Parker, J. D. A. (2000). *Handbook of Emotional Intelligence: Theory, Development, Assessment and Application at Home, School and in the Workplace.* San Francisco, CA: Jossey-Bass.

Bar-On, R., Maree, J. G., & Elias, M. J. (Eds.) (2007). *Educating People to be Emotionally Intelligent.* Westport, CT: Praeger.

Bharwaney, G., Bar-On, R., & MacKinlay, A. (2007). *EQ and the Bottom Line: Emotional Intelligence Increases Individual Occupational Performance, Leadership and Organisational Productivity.* Ampthill, Bedfordshire: Ei World.

Bloom, G., Castagna, C., Moir, E., & Warren, B. (2005). *Blended Coaching: Skills and Strategies to Support Principal Development.* Thousand Oaks, CA: Corwin Press.

Bush, T. (2011). *Theories of Educational Leadership & Management* (4th edn). London: Sage.

Centre for the Use of Research and Evidence in Education (2004–2005). *Mentoring and Coaching for Learning: Summary Report of the Mentoring and Coaching CPD Capacity Building Project.* London: CUREE.

Creasy, J. & Paterson, F. (2005). *Leading Coaching in Schools.* National College for School Leadership. Nottingham: NCSL.

de Haan, E. (2008). *Relational Coaching: Journeys towards Mastering One-to-one Learning.* Chichester: Wiley.

Fitzsimmons, G. & Guise, S. (2010). Coaching for leadership style. In: J. Passmore (Ed.), *Leadership Coaching: Working with Leaders to Develop Elite Performance* (pp. 229–244). London: Kogan Page.

Fullan, M. (1992). *What's Worth Fighting for in Headship?* Maidenhead: Open University Press.

Fullan, M. (2003). *The Moral Imperative of School Leadership.* London: Corwin Press.

Furnham, A. (2010). Coaching for Icarus leadership: helping leaders who can potentially derail. In: J. Passmore (Ed.), *Leadership Coaching: Working with Leaders to Develop Elite Performance* (pp. 115–131). London: Kogan Page.

Goleman, D. (1995). *Emotional Intelligence.* New York: Bantam.

Goleman, D. (1998). *Working with Emotional Intelligence.* New York: Bantam.

Goleman, D. (2000). Leadership that gets results. *Harvard Business Review, November–December*: 93–102.

Howson, J., & Sprigade, A. (2010). *16th Annual Report: The State of the Labour Market for Senior Staff in Schools in England and Wales.* London: National Association for Head Teachers.

Luft, J. & Ingham, H. (1955). The Johari window, a graphic model of interpersonal awareness. *Proceedings of the Western Training Laboratory in Group Development.* Los Angeles, CA: UCLA.

Passmore, J. (Ed.) (2010). *Leadership Coaching: Working with Leaders to Develop Elite Performance.* London: Kogan Page.

Perks, J., & Bar-On, R. (2010). Coaching for emotionally intelligent leadership. In: J. Passmore (Ed.), *Leadership Coaching: Working with Leaders to Develop Elite Performance* (pp. 55–74). London: Kogan Page.

Robertson, J. (2008). *Coaching Educational Leadership: Building Leadership Capacity through Partnership.* London: Sage.

Sergiovanni, T. J., & Starratt, R. J. (2002). *Supervision: A Redefinition* (7th edn). New York: McGraw-Hill.

Taylor, P. R. (2007). *Motivating your Team: Coaching for Performance in Schools.* London: Paul Chapman.

# CHAPTER THREE

# Coaching in primary or elementary schools

*Mary Briggs and Christian van Nieuwerburgh*

## Introduction

As educational organisations embrace coaching as an approach and integrate it into their daily practice, there has been a tendency to focus on secondary and further education. In these contexts, the idea of equipping staff and students with coaching skills and providing one-to-one support for career planning is well received. It is also used as an intervention strategy for both students and staff as can be seen in other chapters in this book. What about coaching in primary and elementary schools? This chapter explores the possible advantages of coaching in this sector. We consider some of the existing research before sharing some of the emerging practice in primary and elementary schools.

Many of the perceived advantages of coaching approaches apply equally to primary and secondary schools. This is particularly true for staff, with strategies such as instructional coaching for teachers working across the age phases (see Chapter Six). One significant difference is in the staffrooms. The primary or elementary school staffroom will always be smaller than those in secondary schools, due to the fact that the average primary or elementary school will necessarily have fewer staff than the average secondary school. This situation has advantages and disadvantages. Many primary or elementary schools flourish as a result of their smaller organisational settings, while others fail to capitalise on this advantage.

There are a number of commonly occurring risks associated with small educational organisations. Fewer members of staff need to cover a broader range of functions and this can mean that there is more solo working in order to meet the demands of all the functions. In smaller organisations, personal disagreements can be more disruptive. Relationships matter more in primary or elementary schools, as staff are less able to avoid those that they find difficult to interact with. On the other hand, the smaller size could mean that staff work together more closely, fostering a team approach to shared responsibilities. Managed well, this can lead to stronger professional relationships that provide mutual support to one another. Primary or elementary schools can operate with a relatively flat management structure and it is easier to undertake whole-school initiatives. This can mean more direct relationships between staff and school leaders, rather than the feelings of remoteness that can occur in larger organisations. Even logistically, it is more straightforward to get everyone together for professional development or strategic planning events. Once a strategy or approach is implemented, monitoring progress and outcomes is more easily managed in a small school.

The other obvious difference between the phases is the age of the students. Broadly speaking, in primary and elementary education, children range from age five to age eleven, while in the secondary phase, students' ages range from twelve to eighteen. Each age group brings its own delights and challenges, and, from a coaching perspective, different ways of engaging directly with students.

As discussed in other chapters in this book, there is increasing interest and innovative coaching practice in elementary and primary schools in the USA, the UK, and Australia. This chapter surveys the range of possible coaching interventions in the primary or elementary school sector. We consider how coaching offers opportunities for peer-coaching, whole-school planning, and formalised coaching arrangements within schools and the wider community. We start by considering how coaching might be used directly with school children.

## Coaching skills and children

Despite the explosion of interest in coaching within the educational sector, coaching with young children is comparatively rare. One piece of research undertaken by Vlach and Carver (2008) focused on the effects of observational coaching on children's graphic representations. Drawings were collected from twenty-two children in a kindergarten once a week for a month. Half of the children received observation coaching that instructed them to look at objects from multiple angles before, during, and after drawing an object; the remaining half of the children did not receive observation coaching. The researchers found that both casual inspection and statistical analyses of data from the videotaped sessions revealed that the coaching was effective in encouraging children to look at objects more frequently during the drawing process. Additionally, each child's drawings were evaluated using a detailed scoring system. This rating system revealed that children receiving observation coaching had significantly greater improvements in drawing scores than children who did not receive coaching. All children receiving coaching had improvements in their drawing scores, with advances primarily involving enhanced detail and conceptual accuracy. This is a focused use of coaching to demonstrate its impact on very specific skills (those of observation) and is in an experimental form rather than part of the educational process at primary or elementary level. In addition, the researchers used an instructional coaching approach that is closer to the directive end of the spectrum (see Chapter Six).

There is little other research in this area, perhaps because young children are not seen as having the maturity to be able to deal with coaching activities as they are influenced by their previous experience and their understanding of terms used. An example of the issues associated with children's understanding of the language comes from one girl of about nine years old. When introduced to discussions about coaching, she immediately associated this with ideas about transport and getting on a bus (Briggs & van Nieuwerburgh, 2011). Young children most often connect coaching with sports or musical skills and predominantly outside education, where many of their chosen activities focus on skills or talents that children have and are, therefore, seen as additional pursuits.

When considering coaching within an educational context, children associate it as part of the skills of the teacher and often describe it as teaching. From research work exploring the development of peer coaching skills with children (Briggs & van Nieuwerburgh, 2011), the words used most often by primary aged children to describe coaching were "training", "helping", providing "tips", "tutoring", "leading", and "teaching". One activity within a workshop suite in this research was for children to draw a giraffe. The children were asked to swap with their partner and give the other person feedback about their drawing, first finding three things they liked about the giraffe, and then one thing that they might change if asked to draw the giraffe again. This approach links to the "three stars and a wish" approach to self-assessment, which was already in use in a number of the classes. Once they had written their feedback, they were asked to swap their drawings back with their partner and allowed time to review the feedback given before moving on to the next activity. The groups then returned to the drawings later in the workshop and had another attempt at drawing a giraffe, taking into account the feedback given. Of a total population of 137, 95% of the children received feedback from their peers during the workshop activities as part of this research, with only seven (5%) not receiving feedback from their peers during one specific activity of drawing giraffes. The majority of children, eighty-seven (63.8%), not only received feedback, but appeared to act upon the feedback given. For a further fourteen children (10%), it was not clear if they had acted upon the feedback or not, with twenty-nine (21.2%) of the participants where it appeared that they had not acted upon any of the feedback given. As it was not possible to follow up each of the participants individually, it might be that the researchers categorised these drawings incorrectly, yet they had to make decisions based upon the evidence from the drawings alone. In this specific case, the children were not given choices about their peer coaches. In addition, owing to numbers of children in classes, some worked in groups of three. Although the workshop did introduce the children to coaching, the main focus was the skill of "giving and receiving feedback" when undertaking specifically chosen activities. We chose to use "fun" activities rather than "academic" tasks in order to avoid the situation of children being too anxious about their academic skills to participate fully in the activities. This work also separated the skills of coaching, in this case "giving and receiving feedback", from the alternative approach of training children as coaches. Although the researchers worked with the oldest children in primary schools (10–11-year-olds), one of the teachers in one of the schools in the sample took the idea and worked on a task in a Year 1 class (5–6-year-olds). In this case, children drew their own faces. They then gave and received feedback from one another. The children were able to give each other feedback on the key features required for drawing faces. An initial observation of the drawings suggests that the children had taken on board the feedback during their second attempt. This suggests that the activities chosen might be applicable across the primary age range.

## Coaching skills and adults

Most often in education it is the adults who act as coaches or mentors in schools. In the primary phase, this is often through staff taking on the role of learning mentors. Even if they do not consider themselves "experts", they have more experience of learning than the children partly just by a factor of age. Learning mentors were introduced to assist specific groups of children to acquire the skills of "learning to learn" through identifying and overcoming barriers to learning. These mentors were often trained teaching assistants within a school who worked with individuals or small groups of children identified as having specific needs to support their learning. These are not necessarily children with special educational needs, but those for whom there are barriers to learning and potential issues around social inclusion. This was a policy response to this issue in the UK at both primary and secondary level of education (Machin, McNally, & Meghir, 2005).

> They often, but not exclusively, have a role that includes an emphasis on looking at emotional aspects of learning, including children's motivation for learning and aspects of their mental world, such as relationships at home, which could be acting as a barrier to learning in the schools setting. (Mintz, 2010, p. 165)

Mintz's research is an initial exploration of how the professional and educational experience that mentors bring to the role affects their perception of their effectiveness and what additional training they would find useful in furthering that effectiveness. In this research, the learning mentors with a background in teaching felt able to set their own working agenda and to negotiate with teachers from a position of confidence, whereas those without this professional background emphasised personal experiences that they drew on in their role. For children, this role within many schools meant they had been identified as in need of some additional support, and it was not offered as a choice, but as something to meet the needs of the adults in changing the children's learning and reaching the required expectations of levels of achievement.

Children view all of these activities as part and parcel of everyday school life, over which they have limited choices. Their responses are bounded by the specific context of the classroom and the expectations of the "ground rules" that are the accepted norms of the situation (Edwards & Mercer, 1987; Simon, 1957). While it is clear that adult coaching situations do have "ground rules", these are negotiated through choices between the participants. Children rarely have choice in relation to their participation in such activities. Furthermore, children also predominantly accept that if they are chosen for a specific group activity, it is as a result of an assessed need they have and would rarely question this in the primary/elementary age group. For teachers trained in the UK, their experiences of coaching approaches start with being mentored as a student when they are allocated a more experienced teacher on their training placements. This mentor takes an overview of their practical training in schools. One mentor can work with a number of student teachers on placement at the same time in a large primary school. While there are variations of the models used, most have a mentor who takes a co-ordinating role in the school, with individual class teachers taking a day-to-day mentoring role for the student teachers working in their classes. Nilsson and Driel's (2010) research is an example of how mentoring can support both the student teacher and the mentor in developing different aspects of their teaching. Their work shows what and how primary science student teachers and their mentors learn from planning and reflecting together on each other's science lessons for pupils aged 7–9. The student teachers had received training in scientific knowledge, but had relatively brief experience of teaching. The mentors were well experienced in the pedagogy of teaching and mentoring, but did not feel confident about their science content knowledge and the teaching of science. Throughout the process of teaching and reflecting together, the student teachers and the mentors expressed several specific examples of their joint learning of instructional and pedagogic content knowledge, as well as knowledge of the children.

The general mentoring approach includes assessment of the student teacher's competences and feedback with targets for each student teacher to work on subsequent placements. There is no choice about who acts as a student's mentor, as this is the school's decision about staff allocated to this role. There is also no choice about working on the targets, as they are linked to the competences for teaching in a primary school. In the UK, these are the standards for qualified teacher status (QTS) (Teacher Development Agency (TDA), 2010), which all students must be able to demonstrate by the end of their training. After completion of the training programme, every teacher undertakes an induction period, usually a school year. It combines a personalised programme of development, support, and professional dialogue, with monitoring and an assessment of performance against the core standards. At the end of their training, they currently complete a Career Entry and Development Profile (CEDP). With the support of the initial training tutor, student teachers identify their starting targets for the induction year. There are two further stages of this process: at the beginning of the induction year with the teacher who will support them in school, and at the end of the year in preparation for their second year of teaching. The process focuses on setting agreed targets for development at key intervals and then leads into the current arrangements for performance management for teachers in the primary sector. Although some higher education institutions offer guidance on mentoring skills for those who work with student teachers, the reality is that any teacher with at least a year's experience might be allocated as a mentor. Placement can be at such a premium that there can be limited consideration of matching the mentor and students and no real choice for the student, even if there is some at the school's end.

In the USA, teacher training is partially delivered through supervised teaching in schools, with a tutor from university and supervision from an experienced teacher, or through an intern programme. These relationships are also described as mentoring approaches, with a clear indication of a more experienced colleague supporting a new entrant to the profession. A key difference is that currently in the USA, this is not linked to the licensing arrangements for teachers to take up posts in state schools. In the USA, researchers such as Gardiner (2010) have been looking at the benefits of peer placements with a mentor as opposed to the more traditional approach of a single student placed with a single mentor in one class. She found that peer collaboration provides important pedagogical scaffolding that helps student teachers to plan and implement complex pedagogies; peer-mentor observation helps student teachers feel more efficacious about their developing practice; sharing responsibility for instruction and distributing roles and resources enables mentors to better meet the needs of student teachers and students; and effective peer placements require mentors to conceptualise their work in different ways. This represents a development of the mentoring approach in initial teacher training that has the advantage of training the student teachers as peer mentors as well as providing development opportunities for an experienced mentor teacher in schools. This is illustrated by the following quote from one of the mentors:

> With two student teachers, they can learn from one another. They have their own level and they can speak more freely with a peer than a mentor. They bounce ideas off of each other, [they] brainstorm . . . they learn and develop together and that collaborative effort allows them to get more from the experience. (Gardiner, 2010, p. 239)

The focus on mentoring rather than coaching for teachers in their early careers will clearly influence their experiences and understanding of the potential differences in the approaches. There were moves towards a coaching model with the introduction of a Masters in Teaching and Learning (MTL), intended to be early career professional development for all teachers. This initiative broke new ground by emphasising a more non-directive coaching approach and by providing training for the school-based coaches. However, during 2010, the funding for this initiative was withdrawn. Coaching and mentoring is also the focus for those engaged in the Teach First programme in the UK. Its intention was to recruit high quality graduates into the teaching profession in their second year. Working with a leadership development officer (LDO) who used coaching and experiential learning techniques, the graduates developed their ability to independently evaluate children's outcomes, identify causes of any problems, and seek solutions, having worked with subject and professional mentors in their first year to develop their initial teaching skills. In this example, the differentiation between mentoring and coaching is about the development of skills from initial skills and knowledge to working towards innovation and leadership. This kind of separation to the terms and use is probably unique to education as a profession.

The decision about whether to call the activity mentoring or coaching can confuse the issue in education, where most of the activities are part of programmes for either children or staff. In education, the majority of such activities are described as mentoring (see Lord, Atkinson, & Mitchell, 2008). Lord and colleagues identified the following areas of impact from mentoring and coaching activities in schools:

- increased reflectivity;
- cross-sector and group working;
- newly trained mentors and coaches (strongest impact);
- organisational culture focused on learning and research;
- reflective and collaborative culture;
- sharing of enhanced knowledge and skills;
- recruitment and retention;
- children and their learning (direct impact).

In our view, the majority of the approaches currently in use in education seem to offer little scope for choice for the participants, regardless of their role. The activities often focus on gaining feedback from others and acting upon the feedback to improve what is seen as a problem. In some cases, this can be about a child not reaching a particular target or level, or controlling the behaviour and management of a class as a teacher. These issues come to the fore when looking at the increase in instructional coaching in the USA. According to the findings of research within the Spokane Public School system,

> coaches are a set of external eyes and a quiet voice on the side. When coaching is successful, the person being coached in a sense *internalizes* the coach's eyes and voice so that he or she can self monitor personal performance. Thus, coaching is for growth—not correction or evaluation. (2004, p. 8)

Although the focus appears to be on the teacher, the overall aim is improvement in children's learning. The coaches are clearly selected for their skills and not just on length of experience.

Instructional coaching has become very popular in the USA as a common form of professional development for teachers at all levels, as discussed elsewhere in this book. This approach appears in a number of different forms and has been used in differing ways across the States. One model shows the focus on school principals having conversations with their staff around the following specific coaching behaviours: attending, active listening, questioning, empathy, feedback, summarising, paraphrasing, and reflective dialogue. Sometimes, this is concentrated on general improvements to the teaching and learning in the classroom, at other times, the focus is on a specific curricular area, such as literacy: for example, L'Allier, Elish-Piper, and Bean (2010) and Powell, Diamond, Burchinal, and Koehler (2010). These two different studies both focus on literacy and the coaching of staff as part of their professional development and the impact on the children's achievement. In the latter study, literacy coaches worked individually with teachers to plan lessons, demonstrate activities, and provide feedback on teachers' implementation of teaching practices presented in intensive workshop training with teachers. This kind of coaching is often seen as a response to a specific need within the schools to raise the achievement in a particular area of the curriculum or to alter behaviour management approaches throughout an institution. In common with the approach taken with the children discussed earlier, members of staff rarely have any choice about their participation in these activities or who is chosen as their coach. The overarching aim is a consistency of approach rather than tailoring the approach of coaching to the individuals involved. Knight (2004), however, shows a variation to this with more choice given to the teachers to become involved in coaching programmes. The key issue appears to be who is driving the agenda for coaching. In some districts in the USA, coaches are appointed by the district to work with staff in schools and these individuals are seen as "experts" selected because of their experience and competence as a teacher offering pre-planning conferences, observation including collaborative planning and model lessons and post conference sessions. At least at the start of the process they are not from the schools' staff, though teachers may choose to train as instructional coaches. One dilemma for this approach is the balance between directing teachers to change their practice and offering them the tools to be able to see the potential changes for themselves.

More recently, there has also been considerable interest in the USA in a non-directive approach called "evocative coaching". According to Tschannen-Moran and Tschannen-Moran (2010), old models of continuing professional development in schools ("telling and selling teachers on how to do things better in their classrooms") have not worked. The authors point out that "it may appear to save time to just tell people what to do and how to do it, with a great deal of urgency and impatience in our voice and body language, but it actually takes more time. And the solutions seldom work" (p. 33). In England, this approach can remind us uncomfortably of the approach of many local authority inspectors who visit schools deemed to be at risk of underperforming. Evocative coaching is described as "a conversational process that brings out the greatness in people" (Tschannen-Moran & Tschannen-Moran, 2010). Taking a humanistic view, the authors start with the premise that "teachers are capable adults who can be trusted to figure out a great many things for themselves; we inspire teachers to change and we partner with them in the change process" (ibid., p. xxi). Fundamentally, this view proposes that the relationship is one of the most important elements of coaching. Evocative coaches connect with educators through strong, mutually respectful, and authentic relationships which recognise each person's strengths and values.

Our view is that the coaching approaches discussed in this chapter represent positive and effective opportunities for professional development, improved relationships, and enhanced learning in primary and elementary schools. Like Tschannen-Moran and Tschannen-Moran, we feel that non-directive approaches can unlock transformational change within schools. In this regard, it is important to ensure that coaching interventions in primary or elementary schools are always voluntary in nature, that the goals discussed through coaching are self-selected, that recipients of coaching have some choice when deciding on a coach, and that a positive approach is adopted.

## Voluntary nature of coaching

One of the reasons that coaching is effective is that the coachee is usually aware of the need for change. People often approach coaches when they are prepared to take steps towards a better future. This makes coaching an ideal vehicle for self-improvement and professional development. Conversely, our experience of working in schools has shown us that imposed change leads to resistance, individually and organisationally. This kind of "forced" change can demotivate staff and leave them feeling de-skilled and disrespected. At the same time, it is fair to say that with the continuous changes to curricula, policies, and procedures having an impact on educational organisations all across the globe, staff in schools need to embrace and lead change in educational practice. Through open, respectful, and honest dialogue with educational professionals, which takes into account their experiences and strengths, it is possible to create the contexts in which real and noticeable change can take place.

## Self-selected goals

This should not be a challenging concept. But for some reason, it is. However, in principle, coaching is all about self-determination. Coachees must select their own goals, and this is important in creating a sense of agency and personal control. Through supported dialogue, educators must set their own realistic goals. This builds self-esteem, increases commitment, and ultimately leads to a higher chance of success. For this to become a reality, an educational organisation needs to have a clear vision of its purpose and aims (more on "Coaching cultures for learning" in Chapter Nine). This allows members of the team to select their own goals within a clear framework and negates the need to "tell them what to do".

## Choice of coach

Another topic that is often debated is the idea of staff being able to choose their coaches. A common argument is that, although desirable, it is not practical or feasible to give staff members a choice of coaches. However, we know that this is of central importance when establishing trust. Boyce, Jackson, and Neal (2010) explore this in detail in their paper which focuses on coaching in the US military. Their work identified three elements that must match between coach and coachee: rapport, trust, and commitment. When these are similarly rated by both parties, the coaching relationships work best. Dobie, Smith, and

Robins (2010) also explore the relationship issues for the choice of mentors for medical professionals, and establish that empathy and understanding of the specialism of the mentee was important for the mentor as was the gender of both parties. While there might be a more limited choice of potential coaches in a small organisation, it is an area that is worth exploring as a group so that all parties can discuss the issues generally before the ground rules are established. Opportunities could emerge for cross-school collaboration, with a number of schools supporting each other through the sharing of coaches.

## Positive approach

Finally, it is commonly acknowledged that changing habits is not easy. It often takes commitment and persistence to change one's own behaviours. Coaching that is offered through a positive and encouraging relationship, we believe, is more likely to support behaviour change than the deficit model. By understanding a person's strengths, values, and aspirations, a coach can build the motivation and energy that individuals need to maintain the change they wish to effect in their lives.

If it is accepted that coaching approaches can make a significant impact on professional learning and classroom practice, how can schools capitalise on the opportunity? The case study of Hayes Park Primary might be helpful in providing one approach to embedding coaching practice in schools (see Chapter Ten). That said, there is no single approach that is suitable for all schools. Every school has their own unique challenges and different starting point. It is important for the whole school community to be involved in choosing to adopt coaching approaches and to agree a shared vision of what will work for individual schools. Below are some questions for you to consider as you work with others to develop the contexts in which coaching and children can flourish.

## How are other primary or elementary schools using coaching?

We believe there are a host of ways in which schools working with young children can use coaching with both staff and students.

Here are some practices that we have observed in primary schools in the UK.

## With staff

- Peer-observation of classroom practice followed by coaching conversations.
- School-based coaches providing a series of one-to-one meetings following a training day to support the coachee to put the new learning into practice.
- Incorporating a coaching element in the performance review process.

## With children

- Development of coaching-related skills such as "active listening", "asking good questions", or "giving and receiving feedback".
- Using a simplified coaching model to support peer assessment.
- School-wide initiative of "catching others being good" where children and staff have opportunities to report "good behaviour", which is then celebrated.

## References

Boyce, L. A., Jackson, R. J., & Neal, L. J. (2010). Building successful leadership coaching relationships: examining impact of matching criteria in a leadership coaching program. *Journal of Management Development*, 29(10): 914–931.

Briggs, M., & van Nieuwerburgh, C. (2011). The development of peer coaching skills in primary school children in years 5 and 6. *Procedia – Social and Behavioral Sciences*, 9: 1415–1422.

Dobie, S., Smith, S., & Robins, L. (2010). How assigned faculty mentors view their mentoring relationships: an interview study of mentors in medical education. *Mentoring & Tutoring: Partnership in Learning*, 18(4): 337–359.

Edwards, D., & Mercer, N. (1987). *Common Knowledge: The Development of Understanding in the Classroom*. London: Methuen.

Gardiner, W. (2010). Mentoring two student teachers: mentors' perceptions of peer placements. *Teaching Education, 21*(3): 233–246.

Knight, J. (2004). Instructional coaches make progress through partnership: Intensive support can improve teaching. *Journal of Staff Development, 25*(2): 32–37.

L'Allier, S., Elish-Piper, L., & Bean, R. M. (2010). What matters for elementary literacy coaching? Guiding principles for instructional improvement and student achievement. *Reading Teacher, 63*(7): 544–554.

Lord, P., Atkinson, M., & Mitchell, H. (2008). *Mentoring and Coaching for Professionals: A Study of the Research Evidence.* National Foundation for Educational Research Northern Office/Training and Development Agency for Schools (TDA).

Machin, S., McNally, S., & Meghir, C. (2005). *Report to the Department for Education and Skills.* London: Excellence in the Cities Evaluation Consortium.

Mintz, J. (2010). Primary school learning mentors: do background and training matter? *Education 3–13, 38*(2): 165–175.

Nilsson, P., & Driel, J. (2010). Teaching together and learning together. Primary science student teachers' and their mentors' joint teaching and learning in the primary classroom. *Teaching and Teacher Education, 26*: 1309–1318.

Powell, D. R., Diamond, K. E., Burchinal, M. R., & Koehler, M. J. (2010). Effects of an early literacy professional development intervention on head start teachers and children. *Journal of Educational Psychology 102*(2): 299–312.

Simon, H. (1957). A behavioural model of rational choice. In: *Models of Man, Social and Rational: Mathematical Essays on Rational Human Behaviour in a Social Setting.* New York: Wiley.

Spokane Public School (2004). The Instructional Coaching Model. Retrieved on 4 October 2010 from www.plcwashington.org/coaching/.../spokane-SD-coaching-model.pdf

Teacher Development Agency (2010). Retrieved on 27 December 2010 from www.tda.gov.uk/trainee-teacher/qts-standards.aspx

Tschannen-Moran, B., & Tschannen-Moran, M. (2010). *Evocative Coaching: Transforming Schools One Conversation at a Time.* San Francisco, CA: Jossey-Bass.

Vlach, H. A., & Carver, S. M. (2008). The effects of observation coaching on children's graphic representations. *Early Childhood Research and Practice, 10*(1). Retrieved on 5 January 2011 from http://ecrp.uiuc.edu/v10n1/vlach.html

# CHAPTER FOUR

# Coaching in secondary or high schools

*Christian van Nieuwerburgh and Jonathan Passmore*

## Introduction

This chapter focuses on how coaching can have a positive impact on secondary schools, 11–18 year old students, and staff. The chapter is divided into three sections. The first section will focus on coaching for enhanced examination performance. Specifically, it looks at recent work undertaken by us to research the impact of a number of different coaching pilot programmes designed to support students and enhance educational attainment. The second section briefly explores the issue of resilience and schools, and how coaching can be used as a tool in secondary schools to address the problem of bullying and stress. The third section of the chapter considers how secondary schools could use coaching with staff to build a learning culture within their school, and explores its wider impact on social skills such as self-awareness, taking greater personal responsibility, and personal confidence.

## Coaching for enhanced examination performance

The UK has seen an enhanced focus on student attainment since 1997. The UK government set targets for individual school performance at

GCSE level (examinations taken at sixteen years) and has used school attainment of A*–C grades at GCSE to inform OFSTED school inspection ratings. Further, grades have become an important factor taken into account by parents in making decisions about which schools they select for their child. This has further encouraged schools to prioritise their performance in examination league tables above other aspects, such as life skills or the development of employability.

The UK coalition government shifted the debate through a further movement towards marketisation of education—the process of encouraging state-owned enterprises to act like market-orientated firms. This has been achieved in the university sector through the removal in the UK of state funding to universities, which meet 80% of teaching costs, and in the schools sector through initiatives such as the introduction of academy status for individual schools. Academy status involves taking schools outside of the local authority education system, with direct funding from central government, and with a sharper focus being placed on schools making the individual selection of students based on direct applications to the school. This agenda has further heightened schools' focus on examination grades at GCSE and A-level, in order to attract student applications and, thus, future funding.

During this period, we have been exploring a number of different models on how to support students in fulfilling their potential. We will briefly review three different models that we have piloted and are evaluating in different schools within the UK. The first model uses professional coaches to deliver coaching to students. The second and third models use a peer coaching approach, with students coaching fellow students towards improved examination attainment.

Our first experience of student coaching was with a project to address borderline GCSE students in the West Midlands (Passmore & Brown, 2009), known locally as ACES. This project employed professional coaches to deliver coaching interventions to students. Coaches were appointed from individuals interested in education, but who were not already trained teachers. These novice coaches received a four-day coaching training programme, as well as completing an enhanced Criminal Records Bureau check before they started in the schools. The four-day programme included training on core coaching skills such as questioning, listening, summarising, and reflecting, as well as problem-solving skills, the basics on how people learn, and managing group behaviour (see Table 4.1). The coaches were also briefed about the objectives of the programme, which was to improve the percentage of students achieving A*–C grade across the local authority area.

Students were identified for coaching using a database (Fischer family trust). The core target for the intervention within this project were students who were not predicted to get five GCSE A*–C grades (the government target for students leaving school), but might be close to doing so. These were considered to be "borderline students". The thinking was that by targeting resources towards students at this level, the overall percentage who achieved five A*–C grades could be increased. At the start of the project, the local authority was below the performance of neighbouring boroughs and below the national target.

Two or three coaches were based in each of the secondary schools in the borough, depending on the size of the cohort identified from the

*Table 4.1.* Topics covered in training programme.

| Core area | Themes |
| --- | --- |
| Developing helping skills | Developing a relationship with a student/coachee |
| | Clarifying student/coachee problems and challenges |
| | Finding solutions and moving the student/coachee forward |
| | How to successfully exit a student/coachee relationship. |
| Learning to learn | The brain's relationship to learning |
| | Mind management |
| | Independent learning |
| | Environmental and behavioural factors |
| | Groupwork to raise achievement |
| | Understanding group dynamics and behaviours |
| | Theoretical models and frameworks |
| | Reflection upon styles and values as a facilitator |
| | Managing boundaries of a group |
| | Practising planning and delivery of group sessions |

database within the school. A total of forty-seven part-time coaches were appointed and subsequently trained in coaching skills. In addition to training the coaches, a communication plan was developed to advise parents, staff, and students about the nature of the ACES project and about coaching. Specifically, the key message was to reassure parents and students that being selected for coaching was a positive step and should not be seen as a remedial intervention.

In total, 1,987 students received coaching over the three years of the project. The average age of the students was fifteen, with each coach working with between twenty and twenty-five students each year. Coaching sessions were generally weekly, and covered topics including study skills, personal problems, and goals. Each coaching session lasted an average of sixty minutes, although this varied between schools, depending on individual school timetables.

The project was tracked year-on-year over a three-year period. This tracking was part of an evaluation programme to assess the impact of the project and review the value for money of the project, which was considered to be a pilot scheme. The project proved popular, with the number of students participating in the project growing from 552 in year one to 772 in year three. The results also show an upward trend, from 53% achieving the required grade in the first year to 73.6% in the third year.

When compared with the local authority's objective, the project made a significant difference in closing the gap between the local authority's overall performance at A*–C grade and that of other local authorities. Over the life of the project, the local authority closed the gap from 6% to 1% within its neighbours and nationally reduced the gap from 16% to 7% (see Table 4.2). This was at a time when all authorities were themselves also making year-on-year improvements in GCSE attainment figures.

In evaluating the overall impact, the evaluation report concluded that the strategy of targeting borderline students at GCSE was a success, and that professional coaches were helpful in enhancing grades in examinations. However, at the end of the three-year pilot, the local authority decided to end the project. The main reason for this was cuts in education funding and the need to focus on core services. While acknowledging the success of the project on borderline students, the local authority felt unable to continue the level of investment required to fund 1–1 student development.

*Table 4.2.*  Results: Local authority's regional and national comparisons.

| Schools | Before project started | (1st year of project) | (2nd year of project) | (3rd year of project) |
|---|---|---|---|---|
| Gap between Local Authority and National Performance Statistical A*–C at GCSE | 16% | 13% | 12% | 7% |
| Gap between Local Authority and neighbouring Local Authority Performance Statistical A*–C at GCSE | 6% | 5% | 4% | 1% |

This experience with professional coaches in the West Midlands led us to reflect on how coaching programmes could be developed for secondary schools and, in particular, to help support examination study at sixteen and eighteen years, but to do so at minimal cost. We considered two options.

The first was to draw on trained coaches to volunteer in schools. This had the advantage of fitting the UK government's Big Society policy while being a low cost intervention and offering high standard coaching from trained coaches. The research evidence suggests that the quality of coach training and the experience of the coach appear to have an impact on the effectiveness of the outcomes. The downside of this approach was that while this might work at one school at one moment in time, with a specific group of parents or supporters, we felt from talking to schools this was unlikely to offer a sustainable model for the long term, as those with coaching skills might switch to paid activities or withdraw support as their child leaves the school.

The second model that we considered involved training students to coach other students. This had the advantage of being low cost, but was also sustainable in that training could be included as part of the school timetable and the trained coaches, who were themselves students, might also benefit from gains in their social and emotional aspects of learning.

As a result, we developed a set of training materials, designed as a three-day coaching skills programme, which could also be divided into nine 60–120-minute lessons. The course covered the basic elements of questioning, listening, summarising, and reflection, as well as covering a structure for coaching conversations—the GROW coaching model (Whitmore, 2002).

Rather than train students ourselves, we took the view that training the teaching staff and providing the teaching resources was the best and most sustainable route to follow. We have now implemented the programme in several schools as pilot schemes, with both teaching staff and educational psychologists attending the training. During this period, the school also works through a logistics plan, which aims to answer the key questions (Table 4.3).

In most schools, the students selected to be coaches were A-level students, with the target students (coachees) as GCSE students. In all cases we encouraged the school to match the coaching intervention group with a control group (based on students expected to get the same grades) to track the impact of the programme in the school. We have also encouraged schools to track the progress of the A-level students in comparison to a similar matched group of A-level students who were not engaged in the coaching programme.

The results from these projects have revealed marginal improvements for both coaches (A-level results) and for coachees (GCSE results). In the one school where we have had a relatively large and

*Table 4.3.* Coaching logistics.

| Key coaching delivery questions to be resolved |
| --- |
| 1.  Which group/year trained as coaches? |
| 2.  How will the coaches be selected? |
| 3.  Which group/year will be offered coaching? |
| 4.  How will coaches be selected if there is more demand? |
| 5.  Is participation as a coachee voluntary? |
| 6.  How will parental consent be obtained? |
| 7.  When will coaching take place? |
| 8.  What happens if coachees don't attend?/How will attendance be tracked? |
| 9.  How long will each meeting be? |
| 10. When will it start and how long will it last? |

stable group of students (over thirty in the coaching group), the results were positive, but were not statistically significant when compared with the control group in respect of the GCSE and A-level results. In this school, the school also tracked the students' attitude towards learning. This, however, did reveal a significant improvement, with the coaching group becoming more positive and receptive towards the learning process when compared with the control group over the life of the project.

In each of the projects to date, we have encountered some logistical challenges in implementing the programme. These problems have related to the challenge of timetabling of GCSE and A-level students, encouraging parents to give consent for their child to engage in a coaching session with a fellow student, and the need to encourage students to continue attending the coaching sessions in the lead-up to the exams. These experiences have allowed us to learn lessons about a greater need for planning in the lead-up to the project, working out in detail the logistics of how, when, where, and with whom coaching happens.

The third model we have explored is the use of peer coaching and mentoring. This involved training school staff to draw on the three-day programme to teach students coaching skills, and from this to encourage students to form a co-coaching relationship with a peer within the same year. The programme design reduces the difficulties of timetabling, when different year groups might be available, but, at the time of writing, we do not have any data on the success or otherwise of the intervention.

In conclusion, the evidence appears to support the wider coaching literature that a professionally trained coach is likely to achieve better results than an individual with a lower level of training. However, within the current financial climate, the use of peer coaches appears to offer a low-cost model which can improve students' social skills, enhance the enjoyment of learning, and facilitate a positive development in the attitude towards learning of students.

## Coaching for resilience: social and emotional wellbeing

Coaching also has a useful role to play in supporting students' wider social and emotional development. As you will see in Chapter Five, there is growing research to show the role of coaching in helping young people to become more resilient, or mentally tough. The research suggests resilience can contribute towards wider goals, such as examination performance.

However, our experience also suggests that resilience can be helpful in reducing bullying within schools. This is not to say that more resilient students are not bullied. Instead, we think the reductions in reports of bullying are due to the interpretation placed on the behaviours of the "bully". Students who are low in resilience might interpret the bullying behaviour in a personal and negative way. They might view the problem as their own. Resilient students might be less likely to see themselves as victims, and more likely to see the bullying behaviour as "stupid" or "child like". In this way, the more resilient student externalises the behaviour and places the responsibility with the bully, who needs to change to become more socially acceptable. By increasing the overall resilience of students in schools, the effect is to reduce the reported number of bullying incidents that take place. While running training courses in resilience is one way to do this, we have been working to develop a self-coaching workbook, which students can use to build their own resilience. As yet, we have not piloted this, but future projects will explore how useful such a workbook is as a mechanism to increase resilience and, thereby, reduce bullying, while improving wider student social skills.

In Chapter Seven, research from Australia is also showing how coaching can play a useful role in the emotional development of students. The results from our own research reviewing examination performance, using a co-coaching approach, suggest that students who were acting as coaches also felt that they had gained from the experience at an emotional or personal level. These experiences emerged during the qualitative part of the research that we undertook when tracking examination performance. The interviews we conducted with students revealed a desire by students to include their coaching experiences on job applications, CVs, and university application forms. The students' belief was that coaching had helped them to think about their own situations. It helped the coach think about their own approach to examinations, which is why there was also some gain in examination performance for coaches. It also helped in personal development, as the coach needed to think about how they were building a trusting relationship with another student, how they would manage confidential issues and how they would demonstrate empathy, while helping the fellow student find their own solution. Of course more research is needed to understand these aspects, but it does suggest that teaching coaching skills and encouraging students to coach each other can have wider social benefits to both the coachee and the coach.

Given these findings, we would argue that there is a legitimate argument for including coaching skills within the social and emotional learning curriculum. Coaching can be seen as a useful life skill that would enhance employability of students, as well as contribute towards the students' wider problem-solving and interpersonal skills. However, before real progress can be made in this area, schools and governments need to recognise the contribution that coaching can make within educational settings.

## Coaching for staff development

Coaching has a significant role to play in staff development within a secondary school setting. We have used it in a variety of ways with partners in schools we have worked with, from supporting career transition to the appointment of a new head teacher or deputy head, staff development for staff in specialist roles, and have witnessed it used in supporting newly qualified teachers as they settle in to the role during their first two years as a new teacher.

The use of coaching to support career transition is well established in the commercial sector. Many newly appointed managers use a coach to help them establish themselves during the first 100 days of their appointment. During this period, key relationships are established and impressions formed which will last throughout the manager's appointment. This is equally true for a secondary school head or deputy. We hold the view that transition coaching is a useful support which governors and head teachers can offer their newly appointed head/deputy. Such coaching can, from our perspective, maximise the chances of success and help the new appointment settle into his or her role.

A typical 100-day transition coaching project might have four to six meetings. The first meeting would normally take place before the head teacher started in their new role and is arranged by governors.

To start the process, we would usually meet outside of the school, and the focus for the first meeting is to build a relationship and consider a plan of action. During this first meeting, we would encourage the head teacher to consider what they wanted to achieve during the early days in the school. We consider the following useful milestones to track and review how things are going:

- milestone 1: first month;
- milestone 2 three month point/first full term;
- milestone 3: first six months/two terms;
- milestone 4: first year/three terms;
- milestone 5: first three years.

A second theme to explore is the head teacher's vision. The coach would encourage head teachers to articulate why they wanted a headship and encourage them to start describing their long-term vision for the school.

A third theme we might explore during this first meeting is the identification of key stakeholders. We would encourage head teachers to consider the key relationships that they would need to form during this initial period and how they would go about forming these relationships. Last, it is helpful to touch on work–life balance, even before a head teacher has started his or her new role. How will the head teacher ensure that he or she can stay energised for the long run? How will he or she manage the role in a way which maintains a balance in life between work and the other tasks that need attention: relationships, family, and social activities?

In subsequent sessions, our experience suggests conversations focus largely on two elements. The first element is supporting the head teacher to develop a coherent plan for his or her school. This plan is likely to consider the financial resources available, the current performance of the school and its staff and students, along with the allies and barriers to achieving this plan. Our experience is that the first 100 days is pivotal in developing this plan as the head teacher comes to understand the school, the staff, students, and the challenges that might not have been apparent during the initial visit and selection process. The second element, which we frequently encounter and which is useful for transition coaching, is to provide a space for confidential discussion and reflection about day-to-day events. As in most senior roles, head teachers do not want to take the pressure of work home with them. Coaching provides a confidential space for a conversation about workplace challenges. It offers the head teacher a space to explore different options, to be challenged about these, and to understand and explore the advantages and disadvantages of each.

Towards the fifth and sixth sessions, we would normally start the process of managing endings. Endings are an important part of coaching; the coach needs to help the coachee to be comfortable moving from the intimate coaching relationship to the professional space. As part of this process, we would encourage the head teacher to find alternative mechanisms for support to replace the coaching relationship. This could be the chair of governors, their partner, their best friend, or a combination of these. However, in building this support team, we will try to help the head recognise that each of these people can play different and complementary roles.

The second area where coaching can make a useful contribution to secondary school life, which we highlighted above, is in the development of teachers in specialist roles. Teachers are taught to train others. They understand the learning process and how best to design and deliver a positive learning experience for their students. However, teachers are not taught how to manage other adults. As a result, taking on a leadership role for the first time can be difficult, stressful, and challenging. Coaching offers an opportunity to discuss, in confidence, line management problems or specialist technical issues. By taking these conversations out of the line management role, the teacher is freed from the anxiety of discussing his or her developmental needs and gaps in knowledge with someone who might subsequently be evaluating their performance. A weekly or fortnightly coaching session for a term can make a real difference in helping the new appointment successfully step up to the expectations of the new role.

The third and final area where we consider coaching can have a real benefit is for newly qualified teachers. While there has been a focus on mentoring over a number of years, coaching, too, can make a useful contribution. The advantage of a mentoring relationship is that a more experienced teacher can help the newly qualified teacher to transfer their learning from theory to practice, share their own knowledge and experience and support the new teacher during the toughest part of their career. Coaching plays a different role. While the mentor offers guidance and advice, the independent coach offers a confidential and objective perspective that encourages the newly qualified teacher to discover for themselves what is most effective. From our experience, a good mentor who is also an excellent teacher can be the best option, but when an excellent teacher is not available, coaching can be a better alternative than a satisfactory teacher who has no experience or training in mentoring.

## Conclusion

In this chapter, we have offered a view about the role of coaching in secondary schools. Coaching, in our view, has an increasingly important role to play in supporting staff and students in secondary and high schools. We are encouraged by the growing range of coaching initiatives and approaches we see in this sector.

## References

Passmore, J., & Brown, A. (2009). Coaching non-adult students for enhanced examination performance: a longitudinal study. *Coaching: An International Journal of Theory, Practice and Research*, 2(1): 54–64.

Whitmore, J. (2002). *Coaching for Performance: Growing People, Performance and Purpose* (3rd edn). London: Nicholas Brealey.

# CHAPTER FIVE

# Mental toughness and its role in the development of young people

*Peter Clough and Doug Strycharczyk*

## Introduction

This chapter focuses on the concept of mental toughness and the mental toughness questionnaire, MTQ48. This concept and approach have emerged from work carried out by one of us (Clough) and Dr Keith Earle at the University of Hull.

Until recently, it can be argued that mental toughness has been widely accepted as a concept but poorly defined. Ongoing development, particularly with the support of coaches and practitioners in a wide range of applications has enabled one of us (Clough) to articulate the concept in a very accessible way. Moreover, the development of MTQ48 has provided a valid and reliable tool to support coaches to achieve better diagnosis of mental toughness (and the potential for evaluation of interventions).

In turn, this had led to identifying interventions that seem to work in developing mental toughness in some sense. A distinct advantage is that many of the interventions are already known to most coaches, tutors, and mentors.

## The origins of mental toughness

To understand the theoretical construction of mental toughness, it is useful to position it within the context of related concepts and theories. The two main contextual constructs are resilience and hardiness, which are rooted in health psychology. Much of the pioneering work on interventions has been drawn from sports psychology. There are also similarities and differences with newly emerging concepts such as positive psychology and the idea of happiness.

Mental toughness is now more usually defined as the quality which determines, in large part, how individuals deal effectively with stress, pressure, and challenge, irrespective of the prevailing circumstances.

We now know that this quality is an aspect of personality and is more of a trait than originally thought. Mental toughness is related to resilience, but is a broader and, in many ways, a more valuable concept for the coach. Much of the recent research into resilience tends to describe it as "the ability to respond positively to an adverse circumstance". Jackson and Watkin (2004) suggest that our internal thinking processes can moderate the impact of adversity and provide a platform from which we can move forward.

The core factors in resilience appear to be the ability to control what can be controlled and to remain committed to achieving some or all of the original goals, despite adversity or setbacks. As we will see, mental toughness embraces these factors and others.

The other key concept relates to "hardiness" (Kobasa, 1979). There has been a significant amount of research to investigate the notion of the "hardy personality", which can be interpreted as a development from resilience. The hardy personality not only copes with adversity, it enjoys the challenge of so doing and will often seek out and "prefer" to operate in a challenging environment.

It is not surprising, therefore, to find that this notion appeals to those engaged in highly competitive activity. In the mid-1980s, an American sports psychologist, James Loehr, first coined the term mental toughness to describe something akin to hardiness (1986) and it has steadily become adopted as the appropriate term for this concept. Loehr was very much a practising psychologist and made no attempt to scientifically test his model or to develop his questionnaire into a psychometric instrument. What emerged, then, was a plethora of definitions and of models that prompted one of us (Clough) to initiate research to fully understand and operationalise this valuable concept.

One very important point to note is that the opposite of mental toughness is not mental weakness. It is mental sensitivity. To put it simply, a mentally sensitive person will often "let things get to them". For a mentally tough person, it will be case of "water off a duck's back". There is no suggestion that mental sensitivity is an undesired state and there is no suggestion anywhere that everyone should become mentally tough. Mentally sensitive people can achieve and they can contribute their own qualities to society and to groups.

## Mental toughness: the model and the measure

The research into mental toughness was largely inspired by the observation that it is possible to place two individuals of equal ability, experience, and development into the same environment and notice that one succumbs to the pressures of stress and performs poorly while the other thrives and achieves high performance.

The difference between the two can be explained through the concept of mental toughness. This explains how individuals develop psychological resilience and an inner drive to succeed. This, in turn, suggests that developing mental toughness is an integral component of effective peak performance development.

One of us (Clough) found that mental toughness has four components, which together provided an overall picture of mental toughness and, therefore, developed MTQ48, the world's first valid and reliable measure of mental toughness. The four components are described in the MTQ48 measure through four scales called the 4Cs: Control, Challenge, Commitment, and Confidence. Two of the scales have subscales.

Individuals' scores are reported on a ten-point sten scale which is based on a normal distribution. Each scale has a high and a low end.

### Control

Individuals who score high on this scale feel that they are in control of their studies, work, and environment in which they work. They exert more influence on what happens around them and are better able to work in multi-tasked situations.

This means, for example, that, at one end of the scale, students will be able handle multiple activities at the same time (e.g., homework, course assignments, etc). At the other end, they might only be comfortable handling one activity at a time.

Ongoing development of MTQ48 has enabled the identification of two subscales to this scale.

- Control (emotion): individuals scoring highly on this scale are better able to control their emotions. They are able to keep anxieties in check and are less likely to reveal their emotional state to other people.
- Control (life): individuals scoring highly on this scale are more likely to believe that they are in control of their lives. They feel that they can deliver their plans and that they can make a difference.

### Challenge

This scale describes the extent to which individuals see challenge and problems as opportunities. Those who see them as opportunities will actively seek them out and will identify problems as ways for self-development. So, for example, at the high end of the scale we find those who thrive in continually changing environments.

Starting a new course, attending a new school or college, or meeting a new tutor is a typical challenge for students. The way the student approaches this will determine how they perform and behave when faced with the challenge. Those whose scores on this scale are low will prefer to minimise their exposure to change and can respond poorly when asked to do so.

### Commitment

Sometimes described as "stickability", this describes the ability of an individual to make a "promise" and keep it (including promises to themselves), despite any problems or setbacks that arise while achieving the goal.

A student who scores at the high end of the scale will be able to handle and achieve tasks to tough deadlines. At the other end, a student might be intimidated by goals and targets and fail to perform.

## Confidence

Individuals who are high in confidence have the self-belief to success-fully complete tasks that might be considered too difficult by individuals with similar abilities but with lower confidence. Less confident individuals are also likely to be less persistent and to make more errors.

For example, students at the high end of the scale will be able to take setbacks (externally and self-generated) in their stride. They keep their heads when things go wrong and a setback could even strengthen their resolve to complete a task. At the other end, individuals will be unsettled by setbacks and will feel undermined by these.

- Confidence in abilities: Individuals scoring highly on this scale are more likely to believe that they are truly worthwhile. They are less dependent on external validation and tend to be more optimistic about life in general.
- Interpersonal confidence: Individuals scoring highly on this scale tend to be more assertive. They are less likely to be intimidated in social settings and are more likely to push themselves forward in groups. They are also better able to cope with difficult or awkward people.

## Mental toughness and its impact in education and the development of young people

In 2007, Damian Allen, Executive Director of Children's and Family Services in Knowsley Borough Council (UK), initiated a series of studies to examine the extent to which mental toughness was a factor in performance and in aspirations in young people (specifically, at that time, those aged about fifteen years old). At broadly the same time, studies in higher education at leading establishments across Europe began to show a close relationship between the mental toughness of students and their employability, their performance, and their ability to complete courses of studies. Initial findings were startling in revealing the extent to which mental toughness is a significant factor in the development of young people. Subsequent work in other parts of the UK and in Holland has consistently confirmed this in every setting.

Mental toughness (as measured by MTQ48) has emerged as a significant factor in the development of young people. Research and well-evidenced case studies show that mental toughness is strongly correlated with the following attributes.

*Performance*

Carefully supervised application of the mental toughness model and the MTQ48 measure in schools, colleges, and universities in the UK, Holland, and Switzerland shows that there is a close link between mental toughness and the performance of young people in examinations. These applications consistently return findings that show around 25% of the variation in a person's performance in exams is explained by the individual's mental toughness.

Developing an individual's mental toughness can translate into better performance. Early small-scale studies in education are beginning to confirm this. An example is the study from Knowsley (UK) with 240 students aged fifteen. The study explored the relationship between mental toughness scores and test performance on verbal ability and quantitative ability tests (SATs).

Figure 5.1 shows how MTQ results were correlated with verbal ability. It is worth also worth noting the parallel lines indicating that

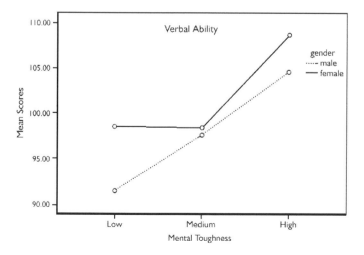

*Figure 5.1.* Mental toughness scores (MTQ48) correlated with verbal ability.

female ability scores are higher than male ability scores. Figure 5.2 depicts how MTQ results were correlated with quantitative ability.

Studies in the occupational world show exactly the same outcomes. As a result, it is likely that mental toughness is also a factor in teacher/tutor performance.

## Well-being

The higher the level of mental toughness, the more the individual is able to deal with the pressures, stressors, and challenges of everyday life. They are able to deal more easily with even the most difficult days. This translates into outcomes such as better attendance, less reporting of stress, and significantly lower reported bullying.

## Aspirations

The work in Knowsley confirmed that the higher the level of mental toughness, the greater the level of the individual's aspirations. This emerges across all studies, but is particularly significant in areas of social and economic deprivation, where "worklessness" can develop. Mental toughness is clearly correlated with aspirations to perform better than the prevailing norm.

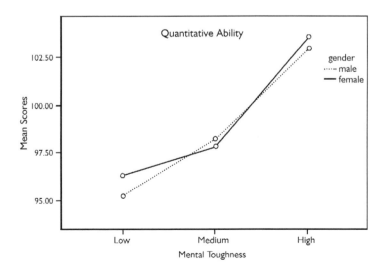

*Figure 5.2.* Mental toughness scores (MTQ48) correlated with quantitative ability.

*Positive behaviours*

The higher the level of mental toughness, the more the individual demonstrates positive behaviours. They will adopt a "can do" attitude, and there is clear evidence that the higher the level of mental toughness, the more likely the student will engage in the class and the school. Again, studies in occupational settings show exactly the same thing.

Curiously, the work carried out in Knowsley showed that many teachers appeared to discriminate between male and female students in terms of engaged behaviour. The same behaviour (e.g., asking questions in class, asking for more explanation, etc.) is often perceived as a "good" behaviour when demonstrated by males but as "troublesome" or "lippy" when demonstrated by females. This appears to be the case whether the teacher/tutor is male or female! Subsequent applications, including in all-girls' schools, show the same phenomenon—highly engaged females are often perceived as troublesome. More research is needed in this area.

*Completion/drop-out rates*

Applications in a number of universities and colleges across the UK show that there is a strong link between mental toughness and the extent to which a student will stick with a programme of study or work and will see it through to its conclusion. There is also good evidence that early assessment of a student's mental toughness and attention to its development is effective in reducing student drop-out rates.

This was confirmed in a project carried out with a leading Swiss-based European Business School, which showed that, contrary to expectations, the mental toughness of new recruits was normally distributed. Around 30% had comparatively low mental toughness (see Figure 5.3). The school had believed that in selecting elite students they would be attracting students with high levels of mental toughness.

The business school experienced a 16% drop-out rate. The study showed that the highest incidence of drop-out came from within this low scoring group, and that identifying those students early and providing pastoral care at an early stage reduced the drop-out rate significantly.

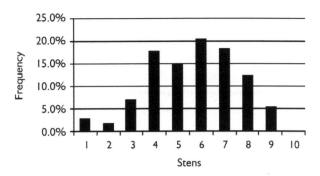

*Figure 5.3.*    Mental toughness.

## Employability

There is a clear relationship between an individual's mental toughness and their ability both to get a job and to get the job they want. People with higher mental toughness scores are more competitive and understand better that job hunting is a competitive activity. This is very clear in Higher Education. There is evidence to show that programmes which focus substantially on qualifications and skills but not emotional resilience do not deliver promised results in terms of employment of students post-graduation.

## Other considerations

Developing psychological or emotional resilience and mental toughness is a very important life skill. As Damian Allen put it, "Not only can we, in many cases, enhance a young person's performance, but these particular skills are useful for just about everything else that person is going to have to do in life."

Returning to the theme of performance, one interesting observation from the early research is that the MTQ48 generally emerges as a better predictor of exam success than the assessment of year tutors. In some ways, this is not surprising. In occupational settings, there is similar evidence that judicious use of psychometrics helps managers to make better decisions about people, even when they have worked with those people for some time and think they already know them well.

It is important to add that tests such as MTQ48 should never be used in isolation. It is most effective when teachers, tutors, and coaches use it with other sources of information to make the best assessment of the person in front of them.

The focus thus far has been on the link between the mental toughness of the student and their performance. As coaches, tutors, and educationalists increasingly adopt the mental toughness concept in their work with students, there is a growing realisation that the mental toughness of those who work with young people is also important. This is as important for parents as it is for teachers.

At one level, this is a straightforward occupational application for mental toughness. There is a plethora of evidence that mental toughness of individuals and groups is closely related to individual and group performance. However, the relationship between a tutor/coach and a student is arguably deeper than an employer–employee relationship. In education, the coachee (student) relies heavily on their tutors and mentors. If the tutor, mentor, or coach "gives up" on the student, the student might also give up.

## Developing mental toughness through coaching

Mental toughness as a concept examines the mindset of an individual when they face challenge, stressors, and pressure. MTQ48 is an instrument that helps to measure that response. This allows the coach to carry out a significant degree of analysis, which is valuable in better understanding the coachee's needs as well as for directing the coach towards appropriate interventions.

Both the model and MTQ48 are very accessible to users and have been designed to be quick and easy to use. The administration can be entirely online. The software is capable of generating reports that provide a generic feedback, coaching ideas, and suggested interview questions to enable the coach to probe an individual's scores.

The whole concept enables:

- diagnosis of individual (and group) needs;
- a framework within which to work with the coachee. Feedback from users suggests that there is high face validity from students—they relate easily to the scales and what they mean for their life in the education process;

- a structure within which they can explore interventions with the coachee;
- the ability to assess progress or change and to evaluate the effectiveness of intervention.

Applying the concept in hundreds of schools, colleges and universities has shown that it is a flexible concept. It can be applied in:

- *Individual coaching or mentoring sessions.* One of the coaches in the original pilot study has evolved an approach that uses feedback from the MTQ48 measure as the basis for a discussion. Instead of feeding back what others think of the student's behaviour and performance, she describes what the report says about the pupil and invites the pupil to provide evidence for or against the suggestion in the feedback.
- *Small group coaching/mentoring.* Several applications show that the concept is an effective approach in small group coaching. This is especially the case if members of the group are similar in terms of their mental toughness in some way. It appears that they might be better able to relate to each other's experiences without being overly judgemental. Usefully, they can be mutually supportive when taking on interventions. When one member of the group "gets it", the rest tend to follow.
- *Large group/whole class coaching and mentoring.* Some development activity is well suited to large group work. Some techniques work better if adopted by whole groups rather than a few individuals.

Other factors which are relevant include the following.

- There is value in "matching" the coach to the coachee. Mentally sensitive coaches are often better at working with mentally sensitive students than mentally tough coaches. They appear to empathise better with the coachee.
- There is also value in examining the characteristics of a group. Raising the expectations and norms of the group can support individual development. Conversely, not doing this can inhibit personal development.

- Assessing mental toughness is valuable in terms of the coachee's approach to the process. Whether it is training, education, or coaching, if the individual does not enter the process in the right frame of mind, they will not get from the process what is being sought. Students with low mental toughness are often "frightened" by the coaching process; it is another source of stress or pressure which is not welcome.

### Interventions

The most effective interventions fall into six broad groupings. Many are drawn from the worlds of sport or occupational psychology (e.g., cognitive–behavioural therapy, neuro-linguistic programming, etc.) where they have been used successfully for many years. Many are well known to teachers, tutors, and educationalists.

However, we also know that, although all these interventions work, they do not all work for all people. There is a need to understand the client better to understand which intervention works best. MTQ48 has a major part to play here.

The six broad groups of interventions are listed below.

- *MTQ48 measure and feedback*: Studies show that pupils with higher than average mental toughness need little further intervention than being told they have mental toughness but that they are at risk of underperforming. Studies show that students with high levels of mental toughness perform better than expected after feedback.
  The original pilot work in Knowsley (described above) showed that pupil Personal Development Reviews can be more effective for all students if these are based on mental toughness feedback.
- *Positive thinking*: Application of tools and techniques such as positive affirmations, thinking of three positives, reframing, etc.
- *Visualisation*: Tools and techniques, including guided imagery, to help pupils envisage better outcomes. Although widely used in sports coaching, it is not used as extensively in education as it might be.
- *Anxiety control*: Tools and techniques based on (muscular) relaxation, controlled breathing, selective use of music, and controlled distraction. These are techniques often used to avoid panic.

- *Attentional control*: Tools and techniques which show students how to improve attention span and maintain focus in the face of distraction. This is probably the least developed area in most schools and colleges, but has the potential to make a significant difference for students.

   Studies show that the attention span for most young people is around 7–10 minutes. But each time we are interrupted, or break from an intellectual activity, we find we have lost up to 30% of our thoughts when we return to that activity. Studying, writing essays, and sitting exams can be tortuous if this is the case. However, it is perfectly possible to increase attention span to forty-five minutes and beyond.
- *Goal setting*: How to set goals, how to balance goals, and how to deal with big goals.

## Evidence for mental toughness

Much of the evidence to date has come from sports and occupational settings. However, since 2007, several major studies have been undertaken in the UK (general population studies, transition into secondary education studies, gifted and talented pupil studies, employability, drop-out rates, etc). Major studies are under way in Holland, Poland, the United Arab Emirates, and Australia to explore the application of mental toughness with young people. Many have already been published as case studies, with several being prepared for peer reviewed journals for future publication.

There are two recent major and independent studies, carried out in Canada and in Italy, respectively, which have helped us develop our understanding of mental toughness, enhancing our understanding of this concept.

The first, from the University of Western Ontario (Horsburgh, Schermer, Veselka, & Vernon, 2009), carried out a study on monozygotic and dizygotic (identical and non-identical) twins who had been separated at birth. The study found that:

- the four scales of MTQ were valid;
- there was evidence for a genetic component, particularly with the "challenge" and "confidence" scales. In other words, some people were born with more mental toughness than others.

The second study, from the universities of Parma, and Modena and Reggio Emilia (Clough, Newton , Bruen, & Venneri, 2010), used MRI technology to examine the brains of eighty individuals who had completed the MTQ48 measure. In summary, the results showed that:

- there was correlation between grey matter density in specific areas of the brain and an individual's mental toughness score, and that this correlation existed at the level of the four scales;
- the known function of these parts of the brain were consistent with the description for each of the relevant MTQ48 scales.

These two studies show that:

- mental toughness is a valid concept and that it has both trait- and state-like qualities;
- there is a biological as well as a psychological explanation for mental toughness;
- there is a hereditary component to mental toughness.

## Research into coaching and using mental toughness

Arguably, one of the core purposes of coaching is the enhancement of an individual's ability to cope effectively with challenges. There are a number of mental toughness research findings that relate directly to this. For example, as would be expected, positive psychological constructs such as optimism have been found to be significantly related to self-reported mental toughness (Nicholls, Polman, Levy, & Backhouse, 2008).

A number of studies have used MTQ48 to investigate relationships between mental toughness and coping. Numerous researchers have emphasised the ability to cope effectively in adverse or pressure situations as being a key component of mental toughness (e.g., Bull, Shambrook, James, & Brooks, 2005; Jones, Hanton, & Connaughton, 2002). In a relatively large study employing 677 athletes, from a variety of sports and different levels of performance, Nicholls, Polman, Levy, and Backhouse (2008) found a number of significant relationships between mental toughness and use of coping strategies. Consistent with theoretical predictions, mental toughness was found to be associated with more problem- or approach-coping strategies (mental imagery, effort expenditure, thought control, and logical analysis), but less use of avoidance-coping strategies such as distancing, mental distraction, or resignation. In other words, tougher individuals were better able to "face up" to their issues.

Building on this work, Kaiseler, Polman, and Nicholls (2009) used MTQ48 and assessed stress appraisal, coping, and coping effectiveness in a study where 482 athletes reported how they coped with a self-selected intense stressor experienced within a two-week period. These researchers reported higher levels of mental toughness to be significantly related to experiencing less stress and more control.

Given that enhancing client control is a major objective of most coaching interventions, the significance of this data is clear. It is quite plausible that enhancing mental toughness will enhance an individual's feelings of control, perhaps allowing them to take more responsibility for their personal development. In addition, measuring mental toughness will allow the coach to assess the amount and type of intervention that is required.

In a very interesting recent study, Crust and Azadi (2009) assessed the leadership preferences of mentally tough athletes using MTQ48. Consistent with theoretical predictions, higher levels of mental toughness were significantly and positively associated with a preference for training and instructive behaviours. This result appears consistent with conceptualisations of mental toughness that emphasise an internal locus of control and a task-orientated focus (e.g. Jones, Hanton, & Connaughton, 2007). Crust and Azadi suggest that this finding probably reflects a commitment to, and striving for, performance enhancement. Tapping into this desire can only help the coach and coachee. This focus on internal locus of control is a major element in many educational environments. Crust and Azadi (2010) have hypothesised a positive relationship between use of psychological strategies and mental toughness.

Three performance strategies were found to be significantly and positively related to mental toughness in both practice and competition: relaxation strategies, self-talk, and emotional control. The small to moderate correlations found by Crust and Azadi appear similar to those reported for mental toughness and coping (Nicholls, Polman, Levy, & Backhouse, 2008) and are in line with trait conceptualisations of mental toughness.

Perhaps most noteworthy were relationships between the subscales of the MTQ48 and the use of psychological strategies. For example, commitment was found to be the subscale most frequently related to use of psychological strategies, which the authors speculated could reflect being deeply committed to one's chosen sport and, thus, seeking out alternative ways of enhancing performance.

By matching interventions with an individual's "coachability profile", it is hoped that a more effective and efficient approach can be utilised. For example, it would be advisable to match goal-setting interventions with the coachee's levels of commitment. In addition, it should be possible to alter the "coachability profile" by altering mental toughness levels. Within the educational domain, it is clear that MTQ48 would allow the coach to more objectively select the intervention to be used.

## Conclusion

In this chapter, the usefulness and value of the concept of mental toughness has been examined. Recent work has shown that mental toughness and the MTQ48 measure are robust and practical developments which provide coaches and mentors in education with a structured and accessible way to attend to a key need in the development of young people: to guide them in learning how to deal with challenge as well as dealing with the stressors and pressures of growing up and optimising their involvement with the education process.

MTQ48 provides a structured approach for diagnosis and provides a means for evaluating change as well as evaluating the effectiveness of different interventions. The application of continuous improvement is needed in coaching as in other areas. With its roots in resilience and hardiness, mental toughness provides a solid basis on which a coach can select and apply interventions to their coachees. Our experience and the experience of coaches in sports and occupational settings show that mental toughness can be developed in individuals and they can, as a result, perform better, enjoy greater wellbeing, and realise their potential.

## References

Bull, S., Shambrook, C., James, W., & Brooks, J. (2005). Towards an understanding of mental toughness in elite English cricketers. *Journal of Applied Sport Psychology, 17*: 209–227.

Clough, P. J., Newton, S., Bruen, P., & Venneri, A. (2010). Mental toughness and brain structure. Poster presented at Organization for Human Brain Mapping (OHBM).

Crust, L., & Azadi, K. (2009). Leadership preferences of mentally tough athletes. *Personality and Individual Differences, 47*(4): 326–330.

Crust, L., & Azadi, K. (2010). Mental toughness and athletes' use of psychological strategies. *European Journal of Sport Science, 10*(1): 43–51.

Horsburgh, V., Schermer, J., Veselka, L., & Vernon, P. (2009). A behavioural genetic study of mental toughness and personality. *Personality and Individual Differences, 46*(2): 100–105.

Jones, G., Hanton, S., & Connaughton, D. (2002). What is this thing called mental toughness? An investigation of elite sport performers. *Journal of Applied Sport Psychology, 14*: 205–218.

Kaiseler, M., Polman, R., & Nicholls, A. (2009). Mental toughness, stress, stress appraisal, coping and coping effectiveness in sport. *Personality and Individual Differences, 47*: 728–733.

Kobasa, S. C. (1979). Stressful life events, personality and health: An enquiry into hardiness. *Journal of Personality and Social Psychology 37*: 1–11.

Loehr, J. E. (1986). *Mental Toughness Training for Sport: Achieving Athletic Excellence.* Lexington, MA: Stephen Greene.

Nicholls, A. R., Polman, R. C., Levy, A. R., & Backhouse, S. H. (2008). Mental toughness, optimism, and coping among athletes. *Personality and Individual Differences, 44*: 1182–1192.

# CHAPTER SIX

# Coaching to improve teaching: using the instructional coaching model

*Jim Knight*

## Introduction

I n the past decade, interest in coaching has exploded in the USA. Coaching is recognised as one way to significantly improve teaching practices and many states, districts, and schools are hiring coaches to deliver professional learning in their schools. However, in their enthusiastic efforts to obtain professional development that makes a difference, some leaders have hired coaches without considering the principles, actions, and contextual factors that have been found to increase coaching success. This chapter provides an overview of each of these topics, with a major focus on instructional coaching (Knight, 2007). At the same time, issues that are relevant to any coaching designed to improve the way teachers teach and the way students learn is considered.

## Growing interest in coaching

Coaching in schools has sparked growing interest for many reasons, two of which are especially relevant: (a) a growing recognition that teacher quality is a critical factor in student success, and (b) an equally growing recognition that traditional forms of professional development are ineffective.

## Teacher quality

Two studies in particular have shown the importance of teacher quality for student achievement. Wenglinsky's (2000) analysis of National Assessment of Educational Progress (NAEP) data identified professional development as an important factor in predicting higher student achievement. For example, Wenglinsky reported that students in mathematics classes taught by teachers who had received professional development in working with different student populations outperformed their peers by 107% on the NAEP. Based on these findings, Wenglinsky concluded that "changing the nature of teaching and learning in the classroom may be the most direct way to improve student outcomes" (p. 11).

In another study of student achievement, Sanders and Rivers' (1996) landmark study of two Tennessee School Districts compared the achievement of students who received three years of instruction from weak teachers with the achievement of students who received three years of instruction from strong teachers. Students taught by highly effective teachers scored more than 50% higher than students taught by less effective teachers, offering compelling evidence that "the single most dominating factor affecting student academic gain is teacher effect" (Sanders & Rivers, 1996, p. 6).

## The failure of traditional professional development

As recognition of the importance of teacher quality has grown, so has recognition of the failure of traditional professional development. For example, the most obvious finding from a review of more than 200 documents related to research on coaching was that traditional professional development does not lead to teacher change (Cornett & Knight, 2009). Indeed, traditional one-shot workshops are sometimes worse than useless, because they foster feelings of frustration among teachers who realise they will never be able to implement the ideas they are compelled to learn on professional development days (Knight, 2000).

## Coaching

As a strong alternative to ineffective traditional training methods, coaching is increasingly being advocated. There are several distinct approaches to coaching in schools, each with unique goals and methods. For example, peer coaching (Showers, 1984) enables teachers to observe and coach each other. Classroom management coaching (Sprick, Knight, Reinke, & McKale, 2006) empowers coaches to use a variety of data-gathering and teaching tools to assist teachers in creating safe and civil learning communities. Content-focused coaching (West & Staubb, 2003), primarily employed by mathematics coaches, focuses on deepening teachers' content expertise and lesson planning. Blended coaching (Bloom, Castagna, Moir, & Warren, 2005) combines several approaches to coaching that coaches and administrators can use to coach teachers.

In addition to those approaches described above, three approaches to coaching are especially common in schools in the USA. Cognitive coaches engage in dialogical conversations with teachers and others, observe them while working, and then use powerful questions, rapport building, and communication skills to empower the staff they coach to reflect deeply on their practices. The term literacy coach is used widely to refer to educators who use a variety tools and approaches to improve teachers' practices and students' learning related to literacy. Finally, instructional coaches partner with teachers to help them incorporate research-based instructional practices into their teaching so that they will teach students in ways that enable them to learn more effectively. Instructional coaching, which has been the product of more than ten years of study by researchers at the Kansas Coaching Project, is the focus of this chapter (see box, below).

## Research

The instructional coaching model discussed here is the result of more than a decade of ongoing study of professional learning. Three studies, summarised below, have yielded especially helpful results. For more information and recent developments, see http://instructional coach.org/research.

Researchers at The Kansas Coaching Project (KCP), a division of the University of Kansas Center for Research on Learning, have been studying coaching for more than a decade. Much of the research has been conducted through Pathways to Success, a partnership between KCP and the Topeka, Kansas School District. Pathways to Success has placed instructional coaches in all middle schools and high schools in Topeka since 1999 and provided a setting for much of the research summarised in this chapter.

Additionally, KCP researchers are partnering with Beaverton, Oregon, and Greeley (Colorado school districts) on an Institute of Education Sciences (IES) funded project studying the impact of instructional coaching on student achievement.

KCP staff provide professional learning and consulting to agencies and school districts in more than forty states in the USA, and several countries across the globe. KCP sponsors workshops and conferences at the University of Kansas and disseminates many resources from its website: www.instructionalcoach.org.

*Study one: partnership learning (Knight, 1998)*

The groundwork for the study of instructional coaching was laid in an experimental study comparing a partnership approach to professional development (PD) with a traditional approach. The study utilised a counterbalanced design (Campbell & Stanley, 1963), with experimental control achieved by giving all subjects all treatments. The results suggest that partnership learning PD, when compared with more traditional PD, was a more effective method for communicating content, engaging participants, and building an expectation of implementation.

*Study two: teacher interviews (Knight, 2007)*

During academic year 2003–2004, thirteen ethnographic interviews (Fontana & Frey, 1994) were conducted with teachers who had collaborated with an instructional coach at Chase Middle School in Topeka, Kansas, in the USA. In each of the thirteen interviews, teachers stated that the model lessons were an essential part of the coaching process. One teacher, typical of the majority, said,

"I think it was very important for her to come in and model it. I think the value of actually seeing it happen is you get to see how it works and how she interacts with certain kids that are real problems . . . It also instills confidence in myself. If we had just sat down and talked, I might have understood that, but seeing it in practice is a whole different thing. I think her value to me has been immense. I probably would have sunk without her." (Knight, 2007, p. 117)

Each teacher interviewed stated that model lessons were essential for their own professional learning.

### Study three: implementation (Cornett & Knight, 2009)

In 2008, fifty-one teachers attended an after-school workshop on a scientifically proven content planning tool teaching routine known as the unit organiser (Lenz, Bulgren, Schumaker, Deshler, & Boudah, 1994). The participants were randomly assigned into two groups: (a) no follow-up, and (b) instructional coaching. Thirty-two research assistants observed the classrooms of the teachers in both groups to determine (a) whether or not teachers were using the unit organiser, (b) whether or not teachers were using the unit organiser with fidelity, and (c) whether or not teachers would continue to use the unit organiser.

The results showed that coaching increased both teachers' use of the unit organiser (91.5 $vs.$ 36.2 observed days) and teachers' quality of implementation ($M = 1.08$, $SD = 1.18$ $vs.$ $M = 2.81$, $SD = 0.81$) for workshop only and workshop and coaching, respectively. Additionally, semi-structured interviews conducted eight to twelve weeks after instructional coaching was completed showed that fifteen of twenty-two coached teachers continued to use the unit organiser while only three of twenty-two of the workshop only group continued to use the unit organiser (Figure 6.1). Thus, coaching increased implementation, quality of instruction, and sustained use of implemented teaching practices.

### The theory behind instructional coaching: partnership

A defining characteristic of instructional coaching, as developed by researchers at the Kansas Coaching Project (Knight, 2007), is the philosophical orientation, or theory that underlies everything a coach does.

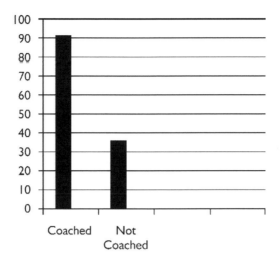

*Figure 6.1.* Evidence of use of the unit organiser.

The term *theory* is used here as it is defined in the *Oxford English Dictionary*, as a "systematic conception or statement of the principles of something". Isaacs has described the important role that theory can play in shaping our actions:

> When we undertake any task, like run a meeting, negotiate an agreement, discipline a child—even meditate—we operate from a set of taken-for-granted rules or ideas of how to be effective. Understanding these tacit rules is what I mean by *theory*. The word *theory* comes from the same roots as the word *theater*, which means simply "to see." A theory is a way of seeing ... Without a theory, however—some way to assess what is happening—we shall be forever doomed to operate blindly, subject to chance. (p. 73)

The theory adopted by instructional coaches affiliated with the Kansas Coaching Project involves a partnership approach, an extension of ideas first stated in the fields of education, business, psychology, philosophy of science, and cultural anthropology. The work of authors such as Paulo Freire (1970), Riane Eisler (1988), Michael Fullan (1993), Peter Block (1993), Peter Senge (1990), Richard Bernstein (1983), and William Isaacs (1999) provides an alternative model for how people can work together. Based on common principles in many of these authors' works, in a separate study (Knight, 1998), these principles were narrowed down to the following seven: equality, choice, voice, dialogue, reflection, praxis, and reciprocity. These seven principles, described below, are at the core of the particular kind of leadership adopted by instructional coaches affiliated with the Kansas Coaching Project.

### Equality: instructional coaches and teachers are equal partners

Partnership involves relationships between equals. Thus, instructional coaches recognise collaborating teachers as equal partners and believe that each teacher's thoughts and beliefs are valuable. As a result, instructional coaches listen to teachers with the intent to learn, to understand, and then respond, rather than with the intent to persuade.

### Choice: teachers should have choice regarding what and how they learn

In a partnership, one individual does not make decisions for another. Because partners are equal, they make their own individual choices and make decisions collaboratively (Block, 1993). For instructional coaches, this means that teacher choice is implicit in every communication of content and, to the greatest extent possible, in the process used to learn the content. As a result, instructional coaches do not aim at making teachers "think like them". Rather, an instructional coach's goal is to meet teachers where they are in their practice and offer choices for learning.

### Voice: professional learning should empower and respect the voices of teachers

All individuals in a partnership have opportunities to express their point of view. Indeed, a primary benefit of a partnership is that it affords each individual access to many perspectives rather than the one perspective of a leader (Covey, 2004; Lawrence-Lightfoot, 2000). Acting on this principle, instructional coaches encourage teachers to express their opinions about content being learnt. That is, they view coaching as a process that helps teachers find their voice, not a process determined to make teachers think a certain way.

*Dialogue: professional learning should enable authentic dialogue*

In a partnership, one individual does not impose, dominate, or control. Partners engage in conversation, learning together as they explore ideas, and reach mutually acceptable conclusions (Bohm, 2000). For instructional coaches, this means that they listen more than they tell. Further, they avoid manipulation, engage participants in conversation about content, and think and learn with collaborating teachers.

*Reflection: reflection is an integral part of professional learning*

Partners do not dictate to each other what to believe; they respect their partners' professionalism and provide them with enough information so that they can make their own decisions (Brubaker, Case, & Reagan, 1994; Killion & Todnem, 1991; Palmer, 1998; Schön, 1987). Thus, instructional coaches encourage collaborating teachers to consider ideas before adopting them. Indeed, instructional coaches recognise that reflective thinkers, by definition, must be free to adopt or reject ideas.

*Praxis: teachers should apply their learning to their real-life practice as they are learning*

In partnership relationships, meaning arises when people reflect on ideas and then put those actions into practice. In a partnership, each individual must be free to reconstruct and use content the way he or she considers it most useful (Bernstein, 1983). For instructional coaches, this means that, in partnership with collaborating teachers, they focus their attention on how to use ideas in the classroom as those ideas are being learnt.

*Reciprocity: instructional coaches should expect to get as much as they give*

In a partnership, all partners benefit from the success, learning, or experience of others; everyone is rewarded by what each individual contributes (Freire, 1970; Senge, 1990; Vella, 1995). For that reason, instructional coaches learn alongside collaborating teachers. Learning about each teacher's strengths and weaknesses while implementing new teaching practices enhances the coach's ability to collaborate with all other teachers and the coach's skill in using the new teaching practice.

The partnership principles provide a way for coaches to organise, prioritise, and choose how they will act. Over the past ten years, researchers at the Kansas Coaching Project have identified seven practices, grounded in the partnership principles, that coaches employ to empower teachers to learn and integrate proven teaching practices. These practices—(a) enrol, (b) identify, (c) explain, (d) model, (e) observe, (f) explore, (g) refine—will be discussed in more detail below.

## The components of instructional coaching

### Enrol

The partnership approach is a highly effective method for enrolling teachers. Instructional coaches taking the partnership approach to enrolling teachers recognise the importance of the principle of choice and view teachers as professionals who are able to decide for themselves whether or not they can benefit from coaching. Indeed, telling teachers they *must* work with a coach can poison the coaching relationship and decrease the likelihood that coaches have a positive impact on the quality of instruction.

Several strategies can be used to enrol teachers (Knight, 2007). For example, coaches can give brief large- or small-group presentations where they explain coaching and identify teachers who are interested in collaborating with them. Coaches and other professional developers can provide an opportunity for teachers to opt in for coaching following any professional development workshop. Also, many teachers are enrolled in coaching during informal conversations with their coach.

Further, principals can refer teachers to coaches by identifying coaching as one option for targeted professional learning based on a specific classroom observation. In essence, this approach holds teachers accountable while respecting their professionalism by providing coaching as one option among many that teachers can choose from to assist with professional growth.

Perhaps the most effective enrolment strategy is for coaches to conduct one-to-one interviews with teachers (Knight, 2007). During enrolment interviews, coaches meet individually with teachers to talk about teachers' successes, roadblocks, and perception of their students' strengths and weaknesses. During such a conversation, the coach explains the practices he/she can share with teachers, and the teacher and coach explore whether or not one of the practices might be valuable for the teacher. We have found that if teachers are likely to resist change, enrolment works best in smaller groups and particularly in one-to-one meetings.

Regardless of the specific enrolment strategy chosen, two important ideas must be conveyed during the enrolment process. First, coaches need to communicate their credibility; that is, their realistic understanding of the opportunities and challenges faced by teachers and their authentic respect for the profession of teaching. Second, coaches need to recognise that people are rarely persuaded by talk; people have to experience success to believe a practice will be effective (Patterson, Grenny, Maxfield, & McMillan, 2008). Therefore, during the enrolment phase, a coach's job is not to persuade teachers that a new practice will be highly effective. Rather, it is to set up an opportunity for teachers to try out a new practice so that they can decide on their own whether or not the practice helps them be more effective with the students in their classes.

### Identify

Instructional coaches can use several strategies to identify the teaching practice they will share with teachers, depending on the teacher's individual interests and needs. This stage is also grounded in the partnership approach, especially with regard to the principles of choice, reflection, dialogue, and praxis. Frequently, coach and teacher identify during an initial enrolling interview a practice to start with. Other options include teachers identifying practices they want to learn during group meetings or asking for support at the conclusion of a workshop. Often, this stage of the coaching relationship starts with the coach observing the teacher's class and then sharing teaching practices that might be especially helpful.

The most important consideration surrounding identification of the teaching practice to be learnt is that teachers truly choose practice that they think will help them be more effective. Little is accomplished when a teacher is not interested in learning the practice being shared by a coach.

## Explain

Once coach and teacher have identified a practice to learn and implement, the coach explains the practice to the teacher. In doing so, the coach's explanations must be (a) precise and (b) provisional. Precise explanations provide comprehensive and easy-to-understand descriptions of exactly how a new practice should be implemented. During the "explain" stage, instructional coaches frequently share checklists and observation protocols to ensure that they clearly communicate how a teaching practice is designed to be implemented.

Being precise is not enough, however. It is important that coaches' explanations are offered using a partnership approach; that is, they must be provisional. Coaches need to explain the teaching practice in a manner that recognises the importance of choice, dialogue, and, especially, reflection in the coaching relationship. Thus, coaches ask teachers to offer their suggestions for how to adapt a given practice to best fit in their classroom. Indeed, coaches explain the practice in a manner that allows the teacher to think along with the coach as they learn the practice.

Coaches adopting the partnership approach do not take a "one-size-fits-all" attitude to professional learning. They assume that teachers want to carefully weigh whether or not any aspect of a teaching practice will work for them, and they provide numerous opportunities for teachers to share their thinking about a practice.

## Modelling

After explaining the teaching practice, instructional coaches ask teachers if they would like to see the practice demonstrated in their classrooms. Again, consistent with the partnership approach, coaches only provide a model lesson if the teacher chooses this option. During more than a decade of experience of coaching teachers through the Kansas Coaching Project, we have found that if the teacher is interested in learning the practice and has co-constructed an observation protocol or checklist with the coach (Figure 6.2), the teacher

**"Cue, Do, Review" Checklist**

Teacher: **Smith** Unit Content: **Science** Date: **3-17-09**

Teacher ID #: _____ School: **Hillcrest** Module: **5**

| TEACHING BEHAVIOR | OBS. | COMMENTS |
|---|---|---|
| **CUE** | | |
| Name the device | ✓ | 100% on task during story |
| Explain how it will help them learn | | |
| Specify what they need to do | | proximity worked. |
| **DO: LINKING STEPS** | | |
| Walk through the device | ✓ | |
| Involve students | ✓ | 70% teacher talk. |
| Shape student responses | ✓ | 30% student talk. |
| Evaluate student understanding | ✓ | majority of hands |
| Re-instruct if necessary | | up during questions. |
| **REVIEW:** | | |
| Ask questions about information | | |
| Ask questions about how the device works | | |

*Figure 6.2.* A completed observation form.

usually welcomes a chance to see what the practice looks like in the classroom.

Just before the model lesson, the coach provides the teacher with a copy of the observation protocol that was finalised during the explanation phase. Then, the coach provides a concise demonstration of the model lesson. This lesson does not need to take the entire length of the class; indeed, it is often preferable to keep the lesson short, so long as the model demonstration is long enough for the teacher to see the new practice. The partnership principles of reflection and dialogue are especially emphasised during this stage. Thus, while the coach leads the class, the teacher notes down her thoughts about the lesson on the observation protocol. Soon after the lesson, the coach and teacher engage in a brief dialogue around the teacher's thoughts about the lesson.

## Observe

After providing a model lesson, the coach offers to observe the teacher implementing the practice and together they have a conversation about how the lesson went. The teacher is usually very agreeable to having the coach observe the lesson since (a) she/he is working with a coach because she/he chose to, (b) she/he is learning a teaching practice that she/he chose to learn, (c) she/he helped to construct the observation protocol and has an opportunity to adapt it if she/he wishes, and (d) the coach has already modelled the practice.

During the observation, coaches use the observation protocol that was used by the teacher when she/he observed the coach. Coaches need to be attentive to areas where the teacher has skipped over aspects of the teaching practice. Even more important, coaches need to be attentive to what went well during the lesson. When coaches report the many effective practices they observe in a class, their comments can be highly encouraging for teachers.

## Explore

As soon as possible after observing a lesson, an instructional coach schedules a follow-up meeting with the teacher to discuss the data that was collected. This meeting is based on the mutual respect between professionals inherent in the partnership principles. Thus, coach and teacher sit side by side as partners and review the data that the coach has gathered. While the coach does not withhold his or her opinion, opinions are offered in a provisional way, communicating that the coach is open to other points of view.

During the collaborative exploration of data, it is important to communicate clearly the genuinely positive aspects of the lesson that was observed. Authentic, appreciative, or admiring feedback must be (a) direct, (b) specific, and (c) non-attributive (Kegan & Lahey, 2001). Simply put, using a partnership approach to coaching, coaches share with teachers what they saw and then, like partners, let them reach their own conclusions.

*Refine*

Rarely is a teacher ready to integrate a new practice smoothly after just one attempt. Coaches provide ongoing support so that teachers are able to maintain use of the new practice and integrate it into their repertoire of teaching methods. At the Kansas Coaching Project, we have found that such support often takes more time than we might initially assume. During the refine stage, coaches adapt their approach to best meet the needs and concerns of each teacher and to best provide support for the individual practices being learnt. Coaches working on unit planning, for example, might spend most of their time in the explanation stage of coaching, whereas coaches sharing a teaching practice that involves a variety of teaching modes, such as reciprocal teaching, might do several model lessons (Table 6.1)

## Building a context for success

Effective coaching does not happen in a vacuum. It is recommend that leaders who want to establish an effective coaching programme consider (a) adopting systems for professional accountability, (b) focusing their professional learning, and (c) aligning the professional learning provided within their schools and districts. Each of these areas is described below.

*Table 6.1.*   Components of coaching table.

| Component | Outcome |
| --- | --- |
| Enrol | Teacher makes a choice to collaborate with a coach |
| Identify | Teacher will choose teaching practice to learn |
| Explain | Both teacher and coach understand teaching practice in detail and construct observation form together |
| Modelling | Teacher is ready to teach using new teaching practice |
| Observe | Coach collects data on how the teacher used the new practice |
| Explore | Coach encourages teacher to continue using new practice; teacher identifies area(s) that he/she can improve |
| Refine | Teacher uses new teaching practice often and well |

*Professional accountability*

The bottom-up partnership approach of instructional coaching is a starting point for improving instruction, but what happens when a teacher who needs to improve chooses not to work with a coach or embrace any form of professional learning? Unfortunately, coaches affiliated with the Kansas Coaching Project have observed that, on occasion, the teachers whom we think would most benefit from instructional coaching are the last ones to choose coaching. What then?

In order to ensure that all teachers engage in meaningful professional learning, schools may benefit from adopting accountability methods that respect teachers' professionalism. In other words, schools and districts should implement professional learning practices that are grounded in the partnership principles but that also ensure that all teachers are involved in continuous improvement of teaching practice. Fullan (2008) and others have referred to this as "top-down and bottom-up".

Administrators can provide top-down accountability for professional learning by conducting teacher evaluations and walk-throughs that focus on particular teaching practices that a school has committed to embracing. Then, principal and teachers can meet to discuss how they might enhance their skills in particular areas. For this conversation to be effective, it is critical that teachers are offered a variety of options so that they can choose the kind of learning that they consider most important, as opposed to being told how to improve (although in some cases it might be necessary for principals to be direct about what area of instruction needs to improve).

For principal evaluations to be effective as a form of professional accountability, principals must be in classrooms frequently, observing teachers either formally for extended periods of time or informally during walk-throughs. Additionally, principals must embrace their role as instructional leaders and have a deep understanding of the effective teaching practices being shared by instructional coaches and other change leaders.

Professional learning communities (DuFour, 1998; Hall & Hord, 2006) is another way to establish professional accountability. To have an impact, professional learning communities must be carefully designed, with (a) sufficient time set aside for teacher collaboration,

(b) care taken to establish positive cultural norms of interaction that are embraced by all, and (c) time used efficiently to focus on useful teaching practices and other concerns that make a difference for teachers.

When teachers develop authentic professional learning communities, accountability arises from peer-to-peer interactions. As powerful as administrator-to-teacher accountability is, peer-to-peer accountability can be even more powerful.

### Sustained, focused, professional learning

School leaders' desire to improve student achievement can prompt them to become over-zealous, promoting too many teaching practices at the same time. As a result, teachers can soon find themselves expected to implement assessment for learning, understanding by design, differentiated instruction, dimensions of learning, positive behaviour supports, content enhancement, and learning strategies instruction all at once, with very little support. Each of these interventions, properly supported, could make a difference to students' lives. But when intervention upon intervention is served up with no attention given to implementation planning, teachers begin to feel overwhelmed by all the competing demands they face, experiencing what Abrahamson (2004) referred to as "initiative overload" (p. 3).

When teachers are facing initiative overload, coaches find it difficult to enrol them in coaching. Professional learning is more effective in settings where educators (administrators and teachers) adopt a focused framework for instruction and target specific teaching practices that everyone will implement. By focusing on a smaller number of high-leverage teaching practices, schools might be able to move forward more quickly than if school leaders propose implementing everything at once.

### Alignment of professional learning

A final factor that can accelerate or impede the success of coaching is alignment of professional learning within a school or district. When teacher evaluations, workshops, professional learning communities, book studies, instructional coaching, and other forms of professional learning target the same high-leverage teaching practices, the various learning opportunities can be mutually supportive, making it easier for everyone involved to implement new practices.

For example, teacher evaluations will probably be most effective when they are tied to specific teaching practices that are also being explored in workshops, professional learning communities, and through coaching. Coaches, of course, stand at the heart of well-organised professional learning. They can facilitate discussion in professional learning communities, offer workshops, and, most important, provide professional support utilising the components of coaching to facilitate the translation of research into practice.

## Three brief cases: a new vision of instructional coaching

To broaden our understanding of what professional learning can be, we shall now look at coaching from the perspective of the coach, the school, and the district.

### Coach

Instructional coach Stacy Cohen, from Topeka, Kansas, has spent more than five years training to be an effective instructional coach. She has attended numerous professional development opportunities offered by the Kansas Coaching Project and attended professional learning opportunities offered by other leaders such as Randy Sprick, a nationally recognised expert on classroom management, and Richard Stiggins, a nationally recognised expert on assessment for learning.

Additionally, over the past six years, Stacy has developed her skills by being coached by project directors from the Kansas Coaching Project. More important, perhaps, she has learnt from her colleagues, whom she observes frequently and who observe her. Stacy and her colleagues also meet frequently to share coaching and teaching practices.

Stacy applies all that she has learnt through these various avenues in her work as an instructional coach. She acts on her deep understanding of the partnership principles. Over time, she has come to collaborate with many teachers, now more than forty a year. Stacy enrols teachers through workshops, one-to-one interviews, and in other ways, and uses checklists to explain precisely how the teaching practices should be taught while leaving room for teachers to tailor the practices to best meet the needs of students. Stacy models the practices, observes teachers, and discusses what she observes until her collaborating teachers are using the practices effectively and habitually. By continuously improving as a coach, Stacy continuously increases the positive impact she has on the lives of children.

## School

In Cecil County, Maryland, at Bohemia Manor Middle School, instructional coach Jean Clark and principal Joe Buckley have worked with their colleagues to focus and sustain professional learning. Jean has attempted to narrow the focus on professional learning, and utilised innovations such as coach-led professional learning communities, where teachers engaged in conversations about video recordings of each other working in the classroom implementing Content Enhancement. Jean and Joe also have met weekly to discuss how they could better work together to align professional learning within the school. Not surprisingly, Bohemia Manor Middle School's students have shown great gains on state student achievement scores, and the school became a model for the district and attracted attention from across the state.

## District

In Greeley, Colorado School District, associate superintendent for instruction Nancy Devine has worked to ensure that the efforts of coaches and principals are aligned within focused professional learning across the district. Coaches in Greeley have received extensive training in coaching, the Houghton–Mifflin reading programme, classroom management, and other high-leverage teaching practices.

Equally important, administrators in the district have received extensive professional learning. Together with coaches, administrators have established guidelines for issues related to confidentiality in the coaching relationship, how coaches use their time, the roles and expectations of coaches, and the nature of the partnership approach to professional learning. Additionally, Nancy has established processes for continuous improvement. Twice annually, administrators meet with an external consultant to evaluate the effectiveness and progress of professional learning in the district. Working with instructional coaches, administrators identify areas in need of improvement, develop action plans for implementing the improvements, and monitor the effectiveness of their implementation plans.

## Conclusion

Improving instruction in schools is a complex and pressing issue. Instructional coaching offers one model for providing professional learning that can have a significant impact on the learning experienced by both students and teachers. When coaches think carefully about their principles and learn proven practices and effective coaching methods, and when schools and districts create a context for professional learning that increases the chance for coaching success, there is great hope for improvement. Most importantly, when coaches help teachers improve the way they teach, children will be more successful, achieving higher scores, enjoying school, and learning more.

## References

Abrahamson, E. (2004). *Change without Pain: How Managers Can Overcome Initiative Overload, Organizational Chaos, and Employee Burnout.* Boston, MA: Harvard Business School.

Bernstein, R. J. (1983). *Beyond Objectivism and Relativism: Science, Hermeneutics, and Praxis.* Philadelphia, PA: University of Pennsylvania Press.

Block, P. (1993). *Stewardship: Choosing Service over Self-interest.* San Francisco, CA: Berrett-Koehler.

Bloom, G., Castagna, C., Moir, E., & Warren, B. (2005). *Blended Coaching: Skills and Strategies to Support Principal Development.* Thousand Oaks, CA: Corwin Press.

Bohm, D. (2000). *On Dialogue.* New York: Routledge.

Brubaker, J. W., Case, C. W., & Reagan, J. G. (1994). *Becoming a Reflective Educator: How to Build a Culture of Inquiry in the Schools.* Thousand Oaks, CA: Corwin Press.

Campbell, D. T., & Stanley, J. C. (1963). *Experimental and Quasi-Experimental Designs for Research.* Chicago, IL: Rand McNally.

Cornett, J., & Knight, J. (2009). Research on coaching. In: J. Knight (Ed.), *Coaching: Approaches and Perspectives* (pp. 192–216). Thousand Oaks, CA: Corwin Press.

Covey, S. (2004). *The Eighth Habit: From Effectiveness to Greatness.* New York: Simon and Schuster.

DuFour, R. (1998). Why look elsewhere: improving schools from within. *The School Administrator, 2*(55), 24–28.

Eisler, R. (1988). *The Chalice and the Blade: Our History, Our Future.* New York: HarperCollins.

Fontana, A., & Frey, J.H. (1994). Interviewing: the art of science. In: N. Denzin & Y. Lincoln (Eds.), *Handbook of Qualitative Research* (pp. 361–377). London: Sage.

Freire, P. (1970). *Pedagogy of the Oppressed.* New York: Continuum.

Fullan, M. (1993). *Change Forces: Probing the Depths of Educational Reform.* New York: Falmer Press.

Fullan, M. (2008). *Six Secrets of Change: What the Best Leaders Do to Help Their Organizations Survive and Thrive.* San Francisco, CA: Jossey-Bass.

Hall, G. E., & Hord, S. M. (2006). *Implementing Change: Patterns, Principles and Potholes.* Boston, MA: Pearson Education.

Isaacs, W. (1999). *Dialogue and the Art of Thinking Together.* New York: Doubleday.

Kegan, R., & Lahey, L. (2001). *How the Way We Talk Can Change the Way We Learn.* San Francisco, CA: Jossey-Bass.

Killion, J. P., & Todnem, G. R. (1991). A process of personal theory building. *Educational Leadership, 48*(2), 14–16.

Knight, J. (1998). *The Effectiveness of Partnership Learning: A Dialogical Methodology for Staff Development.* Lawrence, KS: University of Kansas Center for Research on Learning.

Knight, J. (2000). Another damn thing we've got to do: teacher perceptions of professional development. Paper presented at the meeting of the American Educational Research Association, New Orleans.

Knight, J. (2007). *Instructional Coaching: A Partnership Approach to Improving Instruction.* Thousand Oaks, CA: Corwin Press.

Lawrence-Lightfoot, S. (2000). *Respect: An Exploration.* New York: HarperCollins.

Lenz, B. K., Bulgren, J., Schumaker, J., Deshler, D. D., & Boudah, D. (1994). *The Unit Organizer Routine.* Lawrence, KS: Edge Enterprises.

Palmer, P. (1998). *The Courage to Teach: Exploring the Inner Landscape of a Teacher's Life.* San Francisco, CA: Jossey-Bass.

Patterson, K., Grenny, J., Maxfield, D., & McMillan, R. (2008). *Influencer: The Power to Change Anything.* New York: McGraw-Hill.

Sanders, W. L., & Rivers, J. C. (1996). *Cumulative and Residual Effects of Teachers on Future Student Academic Achievement.* Knoxville, TN: University of Tennessee.

Schön, D. A. (1987). *Educating the Reflective Practitioner.* San Francisco, CA: Jossey-Bass.

Senge, P. (1990). *The Fifth Discipline: The Art and Practice of the Learning Organization.* London: Random House.

Showers, B. (1984). *Peer Coaching: A Strategy for Facilitating Transfer of Training.* Eugene, OR: Center for Educational Policy and Management.

Sprick, R., Knight, J., Reinke, W., & McKale, T. (2006). *Coaching Classroom Management: A Toolkit for Coaches and Administrators.* Eugene, OR: Pacific Northwest.

Vella, J. (1995). *Training through Dialogue: Promoting Effective Learning and Change with Adults.* San Francisco, CA: Jossey-Bass.

Wenglinsky, H. (2000). *How Teaching Matters: Bringing the Classroom Back into Discussions of Teacher Quality.* Princeton, NJ: Educational Testing Service.

West, L., & Staub, F. C. (2003). *Content-focused Coaching: Transforming Mathematics Lessons.* Portsmouth, NH: Heinemann.

# CHAPTER SEVEN

# Positive education programmes: integrating coaching and positive psychology in schools

*Lisa Suzanne Green, Lindsay Gregory Oades, and Paula Lesley Robinson*

## Introduction

This chapter examines the application of positive psychology and coaching psychology in schools. We provide an overview of these fields and research conducted to date. Further, we outline the potential of the combined use of these complementary approaches in the development of larger scale positive education programmes in schools. Positive psychology interventions (PPIs) are described as a practice drawn from the science of positive psychology. Evidence-based coaching, which is based on the theory and research of coaching psychology, is also described, and research supporting its use provided. Suggestions for the integration of positive psychology and coaching psychology are made with a specific focus on applications in the school setting. We argue for a strategic approach to applications of positive psychology and coaching psychology to create positive education programmes that facilitate student, staff, and whole school wellbeing.

## Positive psychology and coaching psychology in schools

Positive psychology and coaching psychology are complementary fields and share common aims and objectives, being the enhancement of optimal functioning and wellbeing. Additionally both could be viewed as fields whose applied interventions fit under the realm of mental health prevention and promotion. In this chapter, we provide an introduction to coaching psychology and positive psychology. We also provide an overview of their associated research to date. This chapter is most relevant to those working in education, although the descriptions of positive psychology and coaching psychology have a broader relevance. This is reflected in the significant interest in both these areas currently within the general community. Both fields are particularly relevant in the school setting, where the ultimate goal is optimal functioning of those working in it, such as staff, and those attending, such as students.

Table 7.1 highlights similarities and differences between these two fields. As can be seen, the primary focus of the science of positive psychology is defining, measuring, explaining, and understanding the factors that have an impact on wellbeing and optimal functioning. Applied positive psychology involves undertaking intentional activities to increase wellbeing (e.g., using strengths in novel ways, cultivating gratitude, practising acts of kindness). While coaching psychology is also concerned with optimal functioning and wellbeing enhancement, in contrast, its focus is on understanding and applying relevant psychological theories and techniques to a collaborative relationship to enhance goal attainment and increase self-regulation for the "normal, non-clinical population" (Grant, 2007). Applied coaching psychology is referred to as "evidence-based coaching". The term "evidence-based coaching" was coined by Grant (2003) to distinguish between professional coaching that is explicitly grounded in broader empirical and theoretical knowledge base and coaching that was developed from the "pop psychology" personal development genre.

It is important to note, though, that coaching psychology has been defined as an "applied positive psychology" (Interest Group in Coaching Psychology, Australian Psychological Society), whereby "coaching" (including the methodology and relationship) also provides the opportunity for the application of positive psychology research, such as strengths identification and use (Linley, Nielson, Gillett, & Biswas-

*Table 7.1*  Similarities and differences between positive psychology and coaching psychology.

|  | Definition | Aims | Established evidence base | Relevance to school education |
|---|---|---|---|---|
| Positive psychology | The science of optimal functioning (Gable & Haidt, 2005) | Enhancement of optimal functioning and psychological wellbeing | Growing—see meta-analysis (Sin & Lyubomirsky, 2009) | PPIs (positive psychology interventions) for the enhancement of student, staff, and whole school wellbeing |
| Coaching psychology | The systematic application of behavioural sicence for the enhancement of life experience, work performance, and wellbeing of individuals, groups, and organisations who do not have clinically significant mental health issues or abnormal levels of distress (Grant, 2007) | Enhancement of optimal functioning and psychological wellbeing | Growing— see annotated bibliography (Grant, 2009) | Evidence-based coaching for the enhance-ment of student, staff, and whole school well-being |

Diener, 2010). The role of positive psychology in coaching has been discussed previously, however further research in regard to its specific applications is much needed (Biswas-Diener & Dean, 2007; Kauffman, 2006; Linley & Harrington, 2005).

This chapter will show that coaching psychology and positive psychology have important roles to play in the school setting as mechanisms to facilitate student, staff, and whole school optimal functioning and wellbeing. Both approaches have primarily been utilised independently and require further integration. Finally, this chapter encourages school leadership and administration to think strategically to create positive education programmes that support and sustain a positive school culture for enhanced optimal functioning of students, staff, and school.

## Positive psychology

Positive psychology was officially launched in the USA in 1998, when Martin Seligman gave his address as President of the American Psychological Association. While it is a relatively new sub-field of psychology, its foundations have a long history. For example, positive psychologists have consistently credited humanistic psychology for pioneering the territory of positive psychological research and practice (Robbins, 2008). Humanistic psychology, launched in the 1950s, similarly articulated the need for psychology as a science to emphasise the "fully functioning individual", and while humanistic psychology continues to be criticised for its lack of scientific validity, Joseph and Linley (2006) claim that positive psychology is a discipline characterised by good empirical science. Positive psychology also has roots in western and eastern philosophical perspectives, including references to Aristotle and Buddha, extending over the last 2,500 years.

Since its inception, scientific research on positive psychology has increased significantly. This has included research on positive subjective experience, positive character traits, and enabling institutions (Seligman, Steen, Park, & Peterson, 2005). Based on this research, positive psychology interventions (PPIs) have been developed which are based on the practical application of positive psychological research. PPIs are intentional activities that aim to increase wellbeing through the cultivation of positive feelings, cognitions, and behaviours. Examples of PPIs include identifying and developing strengths, cultivating gratitude, and visualising best possible selves (Seligman, Steen, Park, & Peterson, 2005; Sheldon & Lyubomirsky, 2006). A meta-analysis conducted by Sin and Lyubomirksy (2009) of fifty-one PPIs with 4,266 individuals revealed that PPIs do significantly increase wellbeing and decrease depressive symptoms.

As the scientific studies suggest, PPIs are promising, but further research is obviously required, particularly in relation to their application with adolescent populations, where the research is still in its formative stages. The majority of research in positive psychology so far has been conducted with adults.

Despite this, interest in applying PPIs with youth and in schools is growing rapidly and empirical research must continue to ensure the application of positive psychology does not overtake the scientific evidence (Norrish & Vella-Brodrick, 2009). Furthermore, Sin and Lyubomirsky (2009) found the success of PPIs to increase linearly with age, emphasising the need for further studies to explore how best to apply PPIs with younger samples.

## Positive psychology in schools

Across the globe, educators, parents, and concerned citizens are asking how we can best prepare our youth for successful adulthood in the twenty-first century (Huitt, 2010). Whilst this has been an age-old question, given the alarming increases in mental illness, youth suicide and societal breakdown, the need has become even greater for learning experiences that allow youth to flourish, lead purposeful lives and contribute to society as virtuous citizens. Schools are now seen as institutions whose role extends beyond academic competence in preparing the whole child (Huitt, 2010). In fact, the focus on schools as a means for preparing young people for adulthood is one of the hallmarks of developed countries (The National Commission on Excellence in Education, 1983).

If people associated with schools solely value the pursuit of extrinsic goals (i.e., high academic scores equals higher education entry equals increased material wealth), then they might inadvertently be supporting misguided ambitions that could lead to disillusionment and self-destruction (Wong, 1998). In contrast, research shows that striving for self-transcendent and sustainable higher purpose through the identification of intrinsic goals (i.e., being a good citizen) leads to increased wellbeing and meaning (Emmons, 1999). Moreover, striving to improve one's own performance, rather than trying to outperform others appears to have greater interpersonal benefits (Poortvliet & Darnon, 2010). Therefore, it would appear that schools have a duty of care to educate their students on the research and application of well-being and optimal functioning interventions.

While the field of positive education might appear relatively new, it, too, has a long history. McGrath (2009) outlined a brief history of "well-being in education" in her keynote presentation at the 1st Australian Positive Psychology in Education Symposium. McGrath (2009) claims positive education arose from a focus on self-esteem in the 1970s, moved to social skills programmes in the early 1990s, then to resilience programmes in early 2000. From then on, it has become a focus on anti-bullying initiatives, values programmes, and student wellbeing initiatives, including social and emotional learning programmes.

Noble and McGrath (2008), on describing "positive educational practices", state that while there have been only limited applications of positive psychology in education, arguably there are many examples of educational psychology practice that are slowly moving away from a deficit model to a more positive and preventative focus on the strengths of pupils, teachers, schools, and families.

While there may be a growing number of schools globally utilising single component or multi-component PPIs (e.g., random acts of kindness interventions), unfortunately, the majority are not being scientifically evaluated. The *Handbook of Positive Psychology in Schools* (Furlong, Gilman, & Huebner, 2009) provides many examples of scientifically evaluated PPIs that schools may utilise as inspiration for evidence-based application in their own school. However, many of these examples are single component PPIs (e.g., gratitude or kindness interventions). A meta-analysis conducted by Sin and Lyubomirsky (2009) found that a "shotgun" approach, in which individuals practise multiple PPI activities, might be more effective than engaging in only one activity (e.g., Fordyce, 1977, 1983; Seligman, Steen, Park, & Peterson, 2005). Accordingly, there is an urgent need for further research on multiple PPIs and whole school programmes, such as the ground-breaking positive education programme conducted at Geelong Grammar in Australia, which, to the authors' knowledge, was not scientifically evaluated. Further research will ensure that the most advanced interventions are being adopted. Reliable and valid PPIs might assist in increasing social and psychological wellbeing and potentially achieve savings in mental health costs.

While examples of multi-component PPIs conducted in schools (which have been scientifically evaluated) are scant, following are a few notable studies. In a multi-component intervention, Seligman, Ernst, Gillham, Reivich, and Linkins (2009) randomly assigned 347 Year nine students (average age of fourteen years) to a year-long positive psychology curriculum or a usual language arts curriculum. The positive psychology curriculum involved activities aimed at cultivating the twenty-four signature strengths included in the Values in Action Framework (Peterson & Seligman, 2004). Individual, participant, and teacher reports indicated that taking part in the PPI was associated with increased engagement with school and improved social skills up to eighteen months post intervention. It is important to note, however, that no long-term significant differences on measures of depression and anxiety were found between the two groups.

More recently, Norrish and Vella-Brodrick completed a study where ninety Year 10 students (average age of fifteen years) were randomly allocated to one of three groups: a six-hour positive psychology workshop, a comparison workshop (that involved young people exploring life's simple pleasures), or a health programme (that integrated usual aspects of the school curriculum such as safe sex and partying responsibly). Participants' wellbeing and symptoms of depression and anxiety were measured post intervention and at seven weeks post intervention. At the time of writing this chapter, the authors were advised that data were still in the analysis phase; however, the findings of this research will provide important information on how positive psychology interventions influence wellbeing and mental health in adolescents.

## Coaching psychology

Coaching psychology is defined as

> the systematic application of behavioural science to the enhancement of life experience, work performance and well-being of individuals, groups and organizations who [sic] do not have clinically significant mental health issues or abnormal levels of distress. (Grant, 2007, p. 23)

This definition clearly demonstrates that the aims of coaching psychology are similar to positive psychology in terms of the outcomes of increasing and understanding optimal functioning and wellbeing, respectively. As an applied positive psychology, evidence-based coaching has been shown to increase wellbeing, goal striving, resilience, and hope in both adults and young people. Studies have shown the approach to be efficacious with senior high school pupils, teachers, public sector managers, and adults generally in both formal (with designated coach) and informal (peer coaching) contexts (Grant, Curtayne, & Burton, 2009; Grant, Green, & Rynsaardt, 2010; Green, Grant, & Rynsaardt, 2007; Green, Oades, & Grant, 2006).

Evidence-based coaching studies include use of solution-focused and cognitive–behavioural approaches, a structured coaching framework, and other key psychological and adult learning theories and models, including the trans-theoretical model of change (Prochaska & DiClemente, 1984), goal setting (Sheldon, 2002), and self determination (Deci & Ryan, 1980). As an applied positive psychology, evidence-based coaching can be utilised to help shift both youth and adults from a languishing to a potentially flourishing state of well-being (Grant, 2006).

Research into coaching psychology is relatively new, and, compared with fields such as clinical psychology, the research base is embryonic. However, there is a growing body of empirical literature suggesting that coaching can be an effective intervention in a wide range of settings and with a wide range of populations (see, for example, Duijts, Kant, van den Brandt, & Swaen, 2008; Franklin & Doran, 2009; Gingerich & Eisengart, 2000; Grant, Curtayne, & Burton, 2009; Grant, Passmore, Cavanagh, & Parker, 2010; Spence & Grant, 2007).

## Coaching psychology in schools

At this stage, there is limited research of applications of coaching psychology and evidence-based coaching in the education sector. However, interest is growing in this field exponentially, with over 2,590 citations in the database ERIC (in October 2010, using the keywords "coaching" and "education") and over 537 citations in the database PsycINFO. It should be noted that the majority of this literature is focused on "academic coaching" for students to enhance learning, or overcome literacy or learning difficulties (e.g., Merriman & Codding,

2008; Plumer & Stoner, 2005). Additionally, there is an emerging literature on coaching for teachers (see Denton & Hasbrouck, 2009) with the increasing use globally of professional coaches in educational settings, with a particular focus on leadership development.

Contreras (2009) conducted a within-subject study of sixty school principals using professional leadership coaches. Results indicated that the school principals reported improved ability to lead their schools. In Australia, conferences such as the Australian Leadership Coaching Conference for Educators, held at Macquarie University, Sydney in 2009, aimed to foster dialogue between researchers and practitioners in the emerging area of educational leadership coaching.

Green, Grant, and Rynsaardt (2007) conducted a randomised waiting list control group study of evidence-based life coaching with an adolescent population. Participants were randomly assigned to receive either a ten-week cognitive–behavioural, solution-focused life coaching programme, or a waiting list control. They found that the twenty-eight female senior high school students in the coaching programme experienced a significant increase in levels of cognitive hardiness, hope, and a significant decrease in levels of depression, compared to the waiting list control group.

Grant, Green, and Rynsaardt (2010) conducted a randomised waiting list control group of "developmental coaching" for teachers. Participants were randomly assigned to receive either a ten-week cognitive–behavioural, solution-focused coaching intervention, or be assigned to a waiting list control. They found that the forty-four high school teachers in the coaching programme experienced a significant increase in levels of goal attainment, wellbeing, and resilience, and a significant reduction in stress.

While these studies provide promising support for the ongoing use of evidence-based coaching in educational settings, further research is required.

*Creating positive schools: strategic applications of positive psychology and coaching psychology*

Positive schools have been defined as ones in which students experience predominantly subjective wellbeing in the form of positive emotions and positive attitudes towards school (Huebner, Suldo,

Smith, & McKnight, 2009). Both positive psychology and coaching psychology can be utilised to enhance wellbeing and optimal functioning and, hence, support the creation of positive schools.

However, despite growing interest both in research and applications of positive psychology and coaching psychology in the school setting, these approaches currently primarily operate in isolation from each other. For example, a school that might undertake "leadership coaching" might not necessarily be engaged in a large-scale "positive education programme" such as that undertaken at Geelong Grammar. Similarly, schools that might have wholeheartedly embraced positive psychology might not have even considered coaching, or be mindful of what it has to offer a school, believing it to be primarily utilised in organisational settings.

It could be argued, though, that both journeys lead to the same destination (i.e., both positive psychology and coaching psychology approaches could lead to increased wellbeing), and, hence, it is not necessary to utilise both approaches simultaneously. For example, if a school were to train staff and students in coaching with the aim of creating a coaching culture (e.g., Hayes Park School, London—see Chapter Ten), research would suggest that this would support enhanced wellbeing of both staff and students. Why, then, would a school need to provide training in positive psychology and offer additional PPIs? Alternatively, why might a school that was interested in creating a large-scale positive education programme (consisting of both explicit and implicit positive psychological approaches), aimed at increasing staff and student wellbeing, require additional education and training in coaching?

We would suggest that while a school may choose to select either approach as a means to create enhanced wellbeing and optimal functioning for both students and staff, it would behove school leadership to consider how a strategic integration of both approaches might provide the best overall approach, particularly in terms of sustainability.

Research has shown that coaching can enhance transfer of training (Olivero, Bane, & Kopelman, 1997). Olivero and colleagues (1997) claim there is a qualitative difference in the type of learning that takes place in training and coaching, with each phase serving a unique purpose. They argue that training provides a period of abstract learning of principles, whereas coaching facilitates specific individual application of learning. Coaching provides the opportunity to practise and obtain constructive feedback regarding the subject matter "learnt" during training. In this case, any explicit training in positive psychology principles could be enhanced through the use of coaching to support the transfer of training and sustain application in daily life.

As such, we would suggest that any school providing training in positive psychology should consider the use of evidence-based coaching as a means to increase retention of knowledge, enhance transfer of training, and be an integral part of a sustainability strategy. For example, if a class of students were to use a lesson learning about "strengths" and then set a goal whereby they could leverage such strengths, the learning becomes personalised and the student takes ownership of the goal. If coaching continued (either on an individual or group basis), there is an additional opportunity to monitor the progress towards the goal. Goals can be set in regard to the application of any positive psychology concept, including gratitude, kindness, forgiveness, etc. Coaching can bring positive psychology to life, whereby the concepts are applied practically to a student's academic or personal life, drawing on the goal-setting and goal-striving methodologies of coaching. A recent pilot study utilising strengths-based coaching for primary school boys has provided preliminary support that participation in such a programme increases levels of engagement and hope (Madden, Green, & Grant, 2011).

As such, we would argue that taking a "coaching approach" to learning and application of positive psychological concepts such as gratitude, kindness, or forgiveness will not only enhance the retention of knowledge by making it personally meaningful, but will also provide a process (occurring within the coaching relationship) whereby students can reflect on their learning (i.e., Kolb's learning cycle, 1984).

Similarly, we would also suggest that a school considering training in coaching for staff or students should also consider simultaneous training in positive psychology to support coaching initiatives. For example, recent research has shown that the explicit use of strengths assessment and use in the pursuit of goals enhances goal attainment and wellbeing (Linley, Harrington, & Garcea, 2010). As noted previously, there is a growing number of articles and resources that provide information on how to integrate positive psychology into coaching. A good example is Biswas-Diener's *Practicing Positive Psychology Coaching* (2010).

Overall, we would suggest there is a need for both explicit and implicit applications of positive psychology and coaching psychology in schools. Explicit applications would include specific education and training for students and staff in the principles of positive psychology and coaching psychology. These classes would not only provide knowledge and skills, but opportunities for practice. For example, Geelong Grammar offers explicit teaching in Year 7 and Year 10 through specific positive psychology programmes (i.e., Penn Resiliency Programme and the StrathHaven Positive Psychology Curriculum). Such education and training on positive psychology or wellbeing provide a psycho-educational approach where staff and students learn the tools and strategies to create a flourishing life. These tools can be applied both in and out of the school setting.

Implicit applications of positive psychology in schools could include teaching methodologies based on the principles of positive psychology, which might be offered through the current curriculum (e.g., using a strengths approach to understand characters in a novel). Similarly, we would suggest that while explicit training in coaching is useful, it is the implicit applications, which might include informal coaching, that support the creation of a "coaching culture".

Clonan, Chafouleas, McDougal, and Riley-Tillman, in their 2004 article entitled "Positive psychology goes to school", claim that important considerations in building positive organisations include (1) operationalising key components; (2) understanding and using the natural environment; (3) planning for sustained change. In terms of operationalising key components, they highlight the importance of clarifying what a positive school environment might look like. We would suggest this involves schools considering how applications of both positive psychology and coaching psychology could help create and enable this vision. In terms of understanding and using the natural environment, they refer to the internal development of programmes rather than the importation of external programmes. This supports the implicit approach to embedding both positive psychology and coaching psychology through the creation of a coaching culture, rather than relying extensively on external training. Finally, in terms of planning for sustained change, they suggest the school needs to build opportunities to practise new behaviours and skills throughout the school. Through the use of a coaching approach, staff and students identify goals where they can explicitly utilise their newfound knowledge of positive psychology. This will lead to generalisation and enhanced sustainabililty of knowledge and skills.

## Future research and implications

Future research needs to extend applications of positive psychology (i.e., PPIs) and coaching psychology (i.e., evidence-based coaching) and, more importantly, on how these two fields might be more closely integrated to enhance outcomes for students, staff, and school. Research on multi-initiative, large-scale positive education programmes is needed, and, as such, the authors have recently initiated such research.

Additionally many PPIs are aimed at a "normal population" rather than a "clinical population", and research on the use of PPIs in clinical settings is currently scant. Such future research needs to address issues such as "mental health screening" prior to undergoing a PPI or evidence-based coaching intervention. There are concerns that without a thorough psychological assessment prior to conducting the intervention, there could be a real danger of a negative outcome, rather than the intended positive one. For example, if school students were to undertake a "strengths-based coaching intervention" and fail to apply their strengths sufficiently or achieve their goals, owing to an underlying clinical disorder such as depression, there might be a danger of worsening the clinical disorder, rather than improving the child's wellbeing.

This issue also applies to coaching, since many coaches assume that those wanting to engage a coach fall within the "normal population". Unfortunately, this might, in fact, be ill founded, as three scientific studies have shown that 25–52% of people attending for life coaching interventions present with significantly high levels of psychological distress (Green, Oades, & Grant, 2006; Spence & Grant, 2007) and 38% of executives presenting for executive coaching similarly report high levels of psychological distress (Kemp & Green, 2010). These mental health or "screening" issues have not yet been raised or discussed adequately within the positive psychology literature or in terms of screening for PPIs. This is an issue that requires urgent research and dissemination to those both providing and seeking either PPIs or evidence-based coaching.

## Conclusion

Both positive psychology and coaching psychology have much to offer schools. To ensure sustainability, though, requires the successful integration and strategic application of both approaches. We have shown how the strategic use by a school of both positive psychology and coaching psychology might increase and sustain optimal functioning for both staff and students. As suggested in this chapter, we would support the creation of a positive education strategy rather than running numerous initiatives that are not integrated. Clonan, Chafouleas, McDougal, and Riley-Tillman (2004) conclude, "no two school systems would implement positive school psychology in an identical fashion" (p. 105). There is, however, a pressing need for further research on such programmes and the need for expert external consultants and educators to work collaboratively with schools to create and evaluate individualised programmes.

## References

Biswas-Diener, R. (2010). *Practicing Positive Psychology Coaching: Assessment, Diagnosis, and Intervention.* New York: John Wiley.

Biswas-Diener, R., & Dean, B. (2007). *Positive Psychology Coaching: Putting the Science of Happiness to Work for Your Clients.* Hoboken, NJ: John Wiley.

Clonan, S. M., Chafouleas, S. M., McDougal, J. L., & Riley-Tillman, T. C. (2004). Positive psychology goes to school: are we there yet? *Psychology in the Schools, 41*(1): 101–110.

Contreras, Y. M. (2009). A descriptive study: coaching school leaders for 21st century schools: a new context for leadership development. *Dissertations Abstracts International* Section A: Humanities and Social Sciences, *69*(7-A): 2538.

Deci, E. L., & Ryan, R. M. (1985). *Intrinsic Motivation and Self-determination in Human Behaviour.* New York: Plenum Press.

Denton, C., & Hasbrouck, J. (2009). A description of instructional coaching and its relationship to consultation. *Journal of Educational and Psychological Consultation, 19*(2): 150–175.

Duijts, S. F. A., Kant, I., van den Brandt, P. A., & Swaen, G. M. H. (2008). Effectiveness of a preventive coaching intervention for employees at risk for sickness absence due to psychosocial health complaints: results of a randomized controlled trial. *Journal of Occupational and Environmental Medicine, 50*: 765–776.

Emmons, R. A. (1999). *The Psychology of Ultimate Concerns: Motivation and Spirituality in Personality.* New York: Guilford Press.

Fordyce, M. W. (1977). Development of a program to increase happiness. *Journal of Counseling Psychology, 24*: 511–521.

Fordyce, M. W. (1983). A program to increase happiness: further studies. *Journal of Counseling Psychology, 30*: 483–498.

Franklin, J., & Doran, J. (2009). Does all coaching enhance objective performance independently evaluated by blind assessors? The importance of the coaching model and content. *International Coaching Psychology Review, 4*(2): 126–144.

Furlong, M., Gilman, R., & Huebner, S. (Eds.) (2009). *Handbook of Positive Psychology in Schools.* New York: Routledge.

Gable, S. L., & Haidt, J. (2005). What (and why) is positive psychology? *Review of General Psychology, 9*: 103–110.

Gingerich, W., & Eisengart, S. (2000). Solution-focused brief therapy: a review of outcome research. *Family Process, 39*(4): 477–496.

Grant, A. M. (2003). The impact of life coaching on goal attainment, metacognition and mental health. *Social Behaviour and Personality, 31*: 253–264.

Grant, A. M. (2006). A personal perspective on professional coaching and the development of coaching psychology. *International Coaching Psychology Review, 1*(1): 12–22.

Grant, A. M. (2007). A model of goal striving and mental health for coaching populations. *International Coaching Psychology Review, 2*(3): 248–262.

Grant, A. M., Curtayne, L., & Burton, G. (2009). Executive coaching enhances goal attainment, resilience and workplace well-being: a randomised controlled study. *Journal of Positive Psychology, 4*(5): 396–407.

Grant, A. M., Green, L. S., & Rynsaardt, J. (2007). Evidence-based life coaching for senior high school students: building hardiness and hope. *International Coaching Psychology Review, 2*(1): 24–32.

Grant, A. M., Passmore, J., Cavanagh, M. J., & Parker, H. (2010). The state of play in coaching today: a comprehensive review of the field. *International Review of Industrial and Organisational Psychology, 25*: 125–168.

Green, L. S., Grant, A. M., & Rynsaardt, J. (2010). Developmental coaching for high school teachers: executive coaching goes to school. *Consulting Psychology Journal: Practice & Research, 62*(3): 151–168.

Green, L. S., Oades, L. G., & Grant, A. M. (2006). Cognitive–behavioural, solution focused life coaching: enhancing goal striving, well-being and hope. *Journal of Positive Psychology*, 1: 142–149.

Huebner, E. S., Suldo, S. M., Smith, L. C., & McKnight, C. G. (2004). Life satisfaction in children and youth: empirical foundations and implications for school psychologists. *Psychology in the Schools*, 41(1): 81–93.

Huitt, W. (2010). A holistic view of education and schooling: guiding students to develop capacities, acquire virtues, and provide service. Paper presented to the 12th Annual International Conference sponsored by the Athens Institute for Education and Research (ATINER), 24–27 May, Athens, Greece.

Joseph, S., & Linley, P. A. (2006). *Positive Therapy: A Meta-Theory for Positive Psychological Practice.* New York: Routledge.

Kauffman, C. (2006). Positive psychology: the science at the heart of coaching. In: D. R. Stober & A. M. Grant (Eds.), *Evidence Based Coaching Handbook: Putting Best Practices to Work for Your Clients* (pp. 219–253). Hoboken, NJ: John Wiley.

Kemp, T., & Green, L. S. (2010). Executive coaching for the normal "non-clinical" population: fact or fiction? Paper presented to the Fourth Australian Conference on Evidence-Based Coaching, University of Sydney.

Kolb, D. (1984). *Experiential Learning: Experience as the Source of Learning and Development.* Englewood Cliffs, NJ: Prentice-Hall.

Linley, P. A., & Harrington, S. (2005). Positive psychology and coaching psychology: perspectives on integration. *Coaching Psychologist*, 1(1): 13–15.

Linley, P. A., Harrington, S., & Garcea, N. (Eds.) (2009). *Handbook of Positive Psychology and Work.* New York: Oxford University Press.

Linley, P. A., Nielsen, A. M., Gillett, R., & Biswas-Diener, R. (2010). Using signature strengths in pursuit of goals: effects on goal progress, need satisfaction, and well-being, and implications for coaching psychologists. *International Coaching Psychology Review*, 5(1), 8–17.

Madden, W., Green, S., & Grant, A. (2011). A pilot study evaluating strengths-based coaching for primary school students: enhancing engagement and hope. *International Coaching Psychology Review*, 61(1): 71–83.

McGrath, H. (2009). An evidence-based positive psychology approach to student wellbeing. Paper presented to the 1st Australian Positive Psychology in Education Symposium, University of Sydney.

Merriman, D., & Codding, R. (2008). The effects of coaching on mathematics homework completion and accuracy of high school students with attention-deficit/hyperactivity disorder. *Journal of Behaviuoral Education*, *17*(4): 339–355.

National Commission on Excellence in Education (1983). A nation at risk: the imperative for educational reform. DHHS Publication No. ADM 065-000-00177-2. Washington, DC: US Government Printing Office (accessed at www2.ed.gov/pubs/NatAtRisk/risk.html on 26 March 2012).

Noble, T., & McGrath, H. (2008). The positive educational practices framework: a tool for facilitating the work of educational psychologists in promoting pupil wellbeing. *Educational and Child Psychology*, *25*: 119–134.

Norrish, J. M., & Vella-Brodrick, D. A. (2009). Positive psychology and adolescent well-being. First Australian Positive Psychology in Education Symposium, Sydney.

Olivero, G., Bane, K., & Kopelman, R. (1997). Executive coaching as a transfer of training tool: effects on productivity in a public agency. *Public Personnel Management*, *26*(4): 461–469.

Peterson, C., & Seligman, M. E. P. (2004). *Character Strengths and Virtues: A Handbook and Classification*. New York: Oxford University Press.

Plumer, P. J., & Stoner, G. (2005). The relative effects of classroom peer tutoring and peer coaching on the positive social behaviours of children with ADHD. *Journal of Attention Disorders*, *9*(1): 290–300.

Poortvliet, P. M., & Darnon, C. (2010). Toward a more social understanding of achievement goals: the interpersonal effects of mastery and achievement goals. *Current Directions in Psychological Science*, *19*(5): 324–328.

Prochaska, J. O., & DiClemente, C. C. (1982) Trans-theoretical therapy— toward a more integrative model of change. *Psychotherapy: Theory, Research and Practice*, *19*(3): 276–288.

Robbins, B. D. (2008). What is the good life? Positive psychology and the renaissance of humanistic psychology. *The Humanistic Psychologist*, *36*: 96–112.

Seligman, M. E. P. (1998). Positive psychology network concept paper. Philadelphia. Retrieved 22 June 2000, from www.psych.upenn.edu/ seligman/ppgrant.html

Seligman, M., Ernst, R. Gillham, J., Reivich, K., & Linkins, M. (2009). Positive education: positive psychology and classroom interventions. *Oxford Review of Education*, *35*(3): 293–311.

Seligman, M., Steen, T., Park, N., & Peterson, C. (2005). Positive psychology progress: empirical validation of interventions. *American Psychologist*, *60*: 410–421.

Sheldon, K. M. (2002). The self-concordance model of healthy goal-striving: when personal goals correctly represent the person. In: E. L. Deci & R. M. Ryan (Eds.), *Handbook of Self-determination Research* (pp. 65–86). Rochester, NY: University of Rochester Press.

Sheldon, K. M., & Lyubomirsky, S. (2006). How to increase and sustain positive emotion: the effects of expressing gratitude and visualising best possible selves. *Journal of Positive Psychology, 1*(2): 73–82.

Sin, N. L., & Lyubomirsky, S. (2009). Enhancing well-being and alleviating depressive symptoms with positive psychology interventions: a practice-friendly meta-analysis. *Journal of Clinical Psychology: In Session, 65*: 467–487.

Spence, G. B., & Grant, A. M. (2007). Professional and peer life coaching and the enhancement of goal striving and well-being: An exploratory study. *Journal of Positive Psychology, 2*: 185–194.

Wong, P. T. P. (1998). Academic values and achievement motivation. In: P. T. P. Wong & P. S. Fry (Eds.), *The Human Quest for Meaning: A Handbook of Psychological Research and Clinical Applications* (pp. 261–292). Mahwah, NJ: Lawrence Erlbaum.

# CHAPTER EIGHT

# Coaching for parents: empowering parents to create positive relationships with their children

*Agnes Bamford, Nicole Mackew, and Anna Golawski*

## Introduction

C oaching for parents has increased in popularity over recent years in recognition of the huge impact that coaching has had in the sports and business sectors. Coaching courses for parents have been successfully delivered in both the corporate world and within schools.

Coaching for parents differs from other traditional parenting interventions in that the coaches are not claiming to be parenting experts, telling parents they are doing something wrong or that they must follow a certain script. The coaching approach focuses on the use of powerful questions to enable parents to understand themselves and their children better; a total belief in parents' ability to succeed; asking instead of telling; the idea that people have the solutions to their problems within them, and that by owning their own solution they will be more likely to implement it.

We share the view advocated by Guldberg (2009) that parents can often feel undermined by media stories and our safety-obsessed culture. Guldberg encourages parents to trust themselves and each other, while believing they can benefit from insights into how they can deal with common challenges of being parents and discover how fulfilling and enjoyable parenting can be.

Parent coaching has not only proved to be beneficial for child development, but also within education and for academic achievements. Coaching methods and skills are easily transferred between parents and teachers, ensuring that children are raised in a consistent manner both at home and school.

By improving the quality of their interactions with their children, coaching can reduce pressure on the parents, making them more effective at work. Many of the skills that parents learn, such as active listening, positive communication, the importance of praise and recognition, are skills that are transferable to the workplace.

Research over recent years has given us insights into the effectiveness of coaching and the results it can achieve (Grant, Passmore, Cavanagh, & Parker, 2010). Even small changes in parents' behaviour or speech patterns can have a significant impact on children's performance and motivation, self-esteem, and confidence.

This chapter looks at the need for parent coaching and its benefits. It offers case studies to illustrate how parents experience coaching, and, finally, it considers how parent coaching has been put it into practice in schools and corporations.

## The need for parent coaching

Berk (2008) has argued that transitions in family life over the past decade, such as a dramatic increase in marital break-up, remarried parents, and employed mothers, have reshaped the family system. Each change affects family relationships and, ultimately, children's development. While family transitions have always existed, they appear more numerous and visible today than in the past. Rapid social change has intensified pressure on the family. Children's well-being continues to depend on the quality of family interactions, which is sustained by supportive ties with carers and community and favourable policies of the larger culture. Thus, Berk highlights some of the key drivers for parent coaching: changing family dynamics, step-families, an increased understanding of the role and impact on parents of long working hours, and less time spent with children.

Parent coach Lorraine Thomas (Thomas, 2005) claims that many working parents fall into the trap of blurring the lines between work and home. They worry at home about what they have not done at work, and vice versa. The problem with this frame of mind is that it increases parents' stress levels in both places. Furthermore, the *Time Use Survey* by the UK's Office of National Statistics (2006) revealed that working parents engage with their children on average for only nineteen minutes a day.

Additional pressures of bringing up a family in the twenty-first century include less freedom and independence for children due to media scares, conflicting advice given through the media, children's access to internet information, and lower expectations about what children are capable of (Guldberg, 2009).

Santrock (2004) emphasises that parenting consists of a number of interpersonal skills and emotional demands, yet there is little in the way of formal education for this task. Most parents learn parenting practices from their own parents, and some of these practices are accepted and others discarded, often without being fully aware that there are other choices. Unfortunately, when methods of parenting are passed directly from one generation to the next, both desirable and undesirable practices are perpetuated, often unconsciously.

A report published by the Children's Society in 2009 advocates that parenting classes should be available to all parents:

> Before a child is born, the parents should be fully informed of what is involved in bringing up a child – not only the physical demands and sacrifices, but the emotional demands and stress as well as the joys which it will bring to their own relationship. The NHS should ensure that parenting classes are available free to all parents around the birth of a child, especially their first. Fathers as well as mothers should be encouraged to take courses in "understanding your child", and be prepared for the strain of sleepless nights, inconsolable crying and financial pressure. (Layard & Dunn, 2009, pp. 28–29)

Although we have established that we do not advocate expert or government interventions dictating to parents how to handle their children, we believe parents can benefit from more awareness about their role and choices and understanding of what is going on for their children. We shall now turn to some of the benefits of parent coaching.

## *Benefits of parent coaching*

According to Wilson (2011), parent coaching gives parents the essential knowledge and understanding of how and why their children react the way they do, thus allowing parents to gain confidence and a better understanding of their role to achieve the mutual respect they want for themselves and members of their family. Furthermore, parent coaching can provide parents with the knowledge, tools, and strategies to effectively support and teach their children as they grow.

Nineteen Minutes, an organisation that specialises in helping working parents make the most of the amount of time they can spend with their families, offers parents coaching skills to generate true quality time. Nineteen Minutes has achieved this through the following focus: "Understanding life from a child's perspective, making the most of every moment spent with your children, building strong, durable relationships and creating memories that will last a lifetime" (www.nineteenminutes.com).

Parent Gym, a non-profit parent-coaching programme in schools located in deprived areas of London and Belfast funded by the private sector, has consistently evaluated the impact of its programmes. Evaluations have shown that parents taking part score 83% higher on standard parenting assessment tests, and their children's conduct problems (assessed by teachers and parents) have fallen by 25% (www.parentgym.com). Parent Gym's support for parents also means that children come into the classroom happy and ready to learn, opening up their chances for success in future life.

The benefits to parents and their children might be obvious, but what about the benefits to the organisations that employ these working parents? According to Nineteen Minutes (2009), organisational gains include increased employee engagement and retention, improved performance, a more fulfilled and productive workforce, a morale booster in difficult economic times, and an improved employer image. In addition, these programmes have a positive impact on attracting and retaining employees. They also suggest staff gain a range of new skills that are transferable to the workplace, such as active listening skills and understanding the impact of providing praise and recognition.

In our opinion, the method of delivery is critical. As with all coaching practice, insight is gained through parents' increased self-awareness. In addition, parents gain an understanding of their own childhood experiences and of the influences of their own parents. This can be achieved effectively, in our experience, through group facilitation, and is enhanced by sharing with other parents. Our experience tells us that there is no "quick fix"; there must be time for self-reflection during the course and creating a "safe space" for parents to explore their feelings. Time needs to elapse between sessions so that participants can practise their new learning and skills.

Parent coaching has proved to be important and successful for both mothers and fathers, in our experience. Research by Nineteen Minutes (2009) highlighted that many fathers felt ill-equipped to deal with the pressure of fatherhood and that parent coaching courses provided them with skills and knowledge that otherwise would not have been easily accessible. In our experience of running corporate courses, a high percentage of the participants are fathers. We have also run exclusive parent coaching courses for fathers with great results.

In our opinion, there are a number of fundamental issues that parents can benefit from exploring, such as giving praise and recognition, encouraging good behaviour, communicating, listening, giving children responsibility and freedom, and the impact of labelling. Psychological research has highlighted why these issues are so important (Wiseman, 2009).

## Praise and recognition

Praise is one of the fundamental needs for children's learning, growth, and development. Parent coaching focuses extensively on the area of praise, as it is recognised as such a pivotal area, yet research has shown that it can be counterproductive if it is based purely on ability rather than effort. Mueller and Dweck (1998) surveyed 400 children aged ten to twelve. They conducted a series of intelligence tests for the children with feedback at each stage. The group of children who received praise for achievement and intelligence were less likely to enjoy the tasks and showed a reluctance to try harder. When children are praised for intelligence, it can produce a temporary feel-good factor, but longer-term it can also induce a fear of failure and make them avoid challenging situations. The children who were praised for effort rather than ability felt encouraged to try harder, regardless of the consequences, and were more motivated to try harder in each stage of the tests. Their research concluded that praising effort encourages resilience, and this is echoed by Hartley-Brewer (2005), who adds that it encourages self-discipline and moral behaviour. Other research by Dweck found similar results among younger children. Hartley-Brewer suggests that children need to be told they are capable in order to flourish and to remember that non-verbal praise such as hugs, smiles, and rewards have a significant part to play.

Matheson (2004) has suggested that if praise is indiscriminate, it teaches children to have lower expectations, which, in turn, reduce motivation. Positive expectations, however, can help develop resilience and coping skills in preparation for future life challenges. Positive expectations also have a significant influence on performance, according to Golawski (2004), who states that through coaching, self-belief in our abilities can be increased. This principle is applied to various aspects of parent coaching to enable parents to support their children's achievements. A positive correlation between expectations and performance is also famously highlighted by Rosenthal and Jacobson (1968).

Hart and Risley (1995) analysed the ways parents interacted with their children to see if *class* was related to intelligence and achievement. They gathered a database of evidence from professional families, working-class families, and families living off benefits. Spoken interactions were recorded as *encouragements* and *discouragements*. They discovered that by the age of three, children of professional families will receive 700,000 encouragements and 80,000 discouragements, whereas a child whose parents are dependent on welfare benefits will experience 60,000 encouragements and 120,000 discouragements. Hence, the need to provide the coaching skills that might not have been learnt naturally by economically disadvantaged parents during their own upbringing. Kline (1998) advocates a ratio of 5:1 for praise *vs.* criticism. This ratio is as relevant in work relationships as within the family. Kline argues that the quality of the attention we give each other is the key to developing an environment that encourages people to think for themselves.

## Encouraging good behaviour (choices and consequences)

One of the key components of parent coaching is encouraging good behaviour and knowing how to manage misbehaviour that adds stress to family life. Parent coaching explores ways of encouraging behaviour so that the parents stay in control and do not resort to physical punishment. It also identifies unconscious "strategies" that children use, and highlights the fact that parents might also be demonstrating some of these behaviours. Steiner (1996) claims that children enter into relationships within their environment by imitation and example. This highlights the importance of parents as role models for their children.

Faber and Mazlish (2001) acknowledge that one of the main parenthood struggles is getting children to behave in ways that are acceptable to us and getting them to co-operate with us. Often, parents report that they are exhausted by the constant battles, trying to get their children to do what they want them to do. They advocate that parents teach children about choices and consequences for their actions, and that parents really notice and acknowledge when children are behaving well. By giving them attention when they are behaving well, they are also getting a fundamental need met—that of attention. Skynner and Cleese (1997) state that children need the opportunity to learn to be good and fit in with society, otherwise they will lose affection, support, and help from others. They should also be encouraged to harness and control the energy expended on tantrums to positive effect in getting what they want.

Freedman (1995) has explored this aspect of child development. The experiment involved a group of approximately forty boys aged seven to ten. They first had to rate the degree to which they liked five toys. Four were relatively cheap plastic toys, but the fifth one was a battery-controlled robot. After rating the toys, Freedman left the room and told the boys that they could play with the cheap toys, but not the robot. Half of the group were told in a gentle manner, whereas the other half were told in a very stern manner. The robot was fitted with a secret device that informed Freedman that all except two of the boys had, in fact, played with it while he was out of the room. One boy had received the gentle approach and the other had received the stern approach. This suggests that both approaches were ineffective in achieving their desired outcome. Six weeks later, a researcher went back for the second stage of the experiment. This time, the boys were asked to draw a picture. The same toys were placed on another table in the room. When they had finished drawing, the boys were invited to play with any of the toys for a few minutes. The biggest difference was that out of the "stern" group, 77% played with the robot, whereas just 33% of those from the "gentle" group played with it. This indicates that a stronger threat gives children an unconscious message that they must really want to do what they are being told not to do. There could be other factors to consider, such as curiosity and rebellion; however, research suggests that although threats might work in the short term, they are counterproductive in the longer term. Steiner (1996) agrees that reprimands give little help at best. In parent coaching courses, we focus on paying attention to the behaviour we want to see more of, which has proved very effective for many parents.

## Communication and listening

To be a good coach in whatever arena, good communication and attentive listening are essential skills. Lucas (2006) argues that the basic principles for effective communication at work apply equally to home and family relationships. There is a correlation between open communication and secure relationships. Poor communication can lead to behavioural problems for children. Good communication needs to be started with children at a young age so that they feel secure and confident in discussing issues later in their teenage years. It would be unrealistic of a parent to expect their child to open up to them later on if they have not experienced attentive listening when they were younger.

Lucas goes on to add that the more you put into attentive listening, the more people will want to talk to you. This will, in turn, lead to fewer misunderstandings. Parent coaching helps parents to learn simple techniques for active listening, such as stopping whatever you are doing and listening intently, communicating with children by getting down to their level and making eye contact with them. One parent commented that by spending just five minutes actively listening to her child first thing in the morning she avoided previous tantrums. Listening skills are transferable back to the business world, so they represent an added benefit for working parents.

Quite often, parents complain that they do not get any feedback from their children. For instance, when they ask "What did you do at school today?", they tend to receive silence or monosyllabic answers. Starr (2008) notes that focused listening enables someone to speak and express themselves. She goes on to say that quality questions that are simple, have a clear sense of purpose, and influences thought or learning without being controlling, are the most effective. One question many parents attending our courses have found effective is: "What was the *best* thing you did today?"

When parents listen deeply to their children and connect on that level, their whole relationship changes, to one of joy, trust, and mutual respect, according to family coach Alan Wilson (2011). When parents allow their children to experience their own independence and self-responsibility, the changes are immense—and it spreads throughout the whole family.

Biddulph (1998) states that we hypnotise children every day though speech patterns and reach into the unconscious mind of children and implant messages. He goes on to recommend that we use positive words that make children competent and give them safe, specific commands to help them think and act positively and be capable in a wide range of situations.

Parent coaching examines the implications of how we speak to our children, and what expectations this creates, and what labels we might be giving children (positive and negative).

## Labelling

Adults can sometimes label children without being aware that they are doing so and without understanding the long-term impact that this could have on them. A powerful exercise by Wearmouth (2000) reviews the labels we give to our children and what expectations and behaviours we might inadvertently be encouraging. Wearmouth goes on to add that the use of labels for disabled children is extremely sensitive and creates associations and prejudices that accompany it. This is supported by Salmon (1995), who states that a special needs label is equated with failure to come up to the mark.

## Responsibility and freedom

Guldberg (2009) advocates the importance of unsupervised play for children's social, emotional, cognitive, and physical development.

Children need to be given space away from adults' watchful eyes, in order to play, experiment, take risks (within a sensible framework provided by adults), test boundaries, and learn how to resolve conflicts. Guldberg (2009) further claims that if children miss out on opportunities for developing a sense of risk and danger and taking more responsibility for their own lives, they are likely to be at even greater risk when later they are let out in the "real world" without having learnt essential skills. Children and young people need to be gradually given more freedom and responsibility so that they have the opportunities to show what they can do on their own.

## How children learn

According to Holt (1991), children tend to learn more easily than adults, and when we better understand the ways children learn, they grow in confidence, knowledge, curiosity, independence, resourcefulness, competence, and understanding. Bruner (1960) emphasised the important role of parents and carers in a child's learning and development process. Bruner shifted his and other learning theorists' focus on the learning process away from school learning only, and included the social conditions in which the child lives and has grown up. This view is supported by Palmer (2006), who concludes that what happens at home profoundly affects children's ability to learn at school. When home and school work in harmony, children have a much better chance of success. From this, it becomes clear that the coaching of parents is likely to have a direct impact on children's learning. Feedback from parents who participated on our courses has demonstrated that attending "coaching for parents" courses has made them feel more able to support their children's learning.

## Overview of a parent coaching course: coaching skills for parents

The parent coaching course was designed and run as three daytime sessions or four evening sessions for both schools and companies, giving parents a chance to practise in between sessions and feed back to the group the changes that they experienced. The facilitators were postgraduate coaches and qualified parent coaching facilitators. They also belong to accredited professional associations and undergo regular supervision

---

*Parent coaching course*

The course covered the following themes:

- Introduction to coaching and its application in family life
- Developmental needs of children—self-reflective memories for parents
- Listening skills—creating the best environment in the home
- How children understand and make sense of the world
- The role of the unconscious mind and the power of language on developing young minds
- Praise, attention and the impact of criticism
- Understanding children's behaviour
- How the need for attention translates into behaviour
- Understanding feelings
- Bringing about behaviour change—useful coaching strategies
- Encouraging good behaviour
- Over-parenting
- The changing face of families
- Investment in emotional well-being for the family
- The power of expectations and living with labels
- Staying in control

---

We have delivered the course a dozen or more times, and received consistent feedback from the parents at the end of each session. Through structured interviews, we have now assessed the impact of the course on three participants 6–18 months after completing the course. We are taking into account the challenges they faced before going on the course, and their achievements following their participation on the course. We also considered the impact on family life and how parents felt attending the course has helped them support their children's learning.

## Case study: Jane

Jane is a mother of two children (aged six and three). Her husband subsequently attended the same course.

> What were the challenges you were facing before attending "Coaching Skills for Parents" and how did you deal with them subsequently?

Jane said what she found most challenging before attending the course was—in her own words—"not having proper quality time with my children for many different reasons. The boys were not wanting to spend time doing what I wanted to do with them, but having their own ideas about how they wanted to spend time with me. Then I'd get irritated, they'd misbehave—or not behave in a convenient manner!! Basically, I did not understand my children, losing touch with them. The course reminded me what it's like to be a child with siblings and how frustrating being a younger member of a family can be. Stopping to see things from their point of view before I react has made life much calmer and more pleasant."

> What have been the key benefits of attending "Coaching Skills for Parents"?

The key benefit for Jane was becoming aware of the distinction between naughty and inconvenient behaviour. "It's not always naughty behaviour; it may just be inconvenient behaviour to the parent." She realises her son might be exploring. Jane feels she is more able to see situations from her child's point of view now.

She is also more aware of her older son's feelings. Jane gained awareness of the impact on herself from being the oldest child in her family, and was able to remember how tough it seemed for her growing up. She now realises how tough it can be for her son being the elder, and is focusing on calming him down, which works very well. Her son is given more time to play on his own at times when he wishes to do so, as it was recognised that this was important to him.

Jane mentioned that the biggest benefit for her husband was awareness around his relationship with his parents and how this was affecting how he was dealing with his own children. He realised that he does not have to transfer to his children practices from his own parents, which he does not necessarily agree with. Through attending the course, he was able to stop and think about how he was bringing up his own children, and realised that we have a choice about doing things differently from the way our parents did.

Taking the time out to do the course, being committed to doing it, and having the opportunity to talk to other people was very beneficial.

Jane says she really enjoyed the course and would do it again. She noticed how strongly she focused on the children during the course and can see the benefits of attending such a course regularly. From other parents she gained insights, including that her children and herself as a parent are not unusual. She also picked up new ideas and useful tips from other parents, including knowledge of cultural differences and how this affects parenting.

What changes have you noticed?

Her elder son (six) talks and shares more than he used to. He is more able to express his feelings and has opened up more than he used to. He is being listened to more by his parents. Her younger son (three) also seems to talk more and is able to express how he feels. "Both boys feel that they have a say, a right to express their opinions, and for it to be taken into account." In the midst of being very busy, the parents are finding out when it suits the children to do something and they seem to be compromising more than before, allowing the children to have more of a say. At the weekends, they have family meetings around the table.

How has attending the course helped you support your children's learning?

The elder son is very competitive (e.g., about his reading level), and Jane says she is more aware of listening to him and taking his concerns seriously. She knows how to take his "problems" seriously and is able to see the situation from her child's point of view. Jane believes the main issue here is about communication, knowing how to talk to the children, encouraging them, and taking their feelings and issues seriously. She has changed her questioning of her son, and now asks questions such as, "What was the best part of your day?" and "What wasn't so good?" and this has made him talk more about what is going on for him.

## Case Study: Susan

Susan is the mother of two children (aged five and three), who attended a corporate course.

What were the challenges you were facing before attending "Coaching Skills for Parents"?

Susan stated that her motivation for attending the course was to find strategies for coping with difficult behaviours such as tantrums. She was keen to understand how she could look at her own behaviour and look at changing in order to manage these issues better.

What have been the key benefits of attending "Coaching Skills for Parents"?

Susan found that when looking at her children's behaviour, she has learnt to take a step back and look at everything else that is going on around her. By taking a look at the bigger picture, asking herself "why are we in this situation?", she was able to recognise that the behaviour is inconvenient rather than "bad", and that the children could simply be hungry or tired rather than naughty.

She now gives them more responsibility and gets them involved in more activities in the home, such as mealtimes and helping around the house. She realises, especially as a working mother, that her children value her time and the more time that she can spend with them, even if it means doing the housework together, is important to the children.

She has started helping them understand the consequences of their behaviour and talks through alternative options if there is a problem. This supports the children to take responsibility for the solution. Susan spends more of her time listening to the children expressing their feelings.

"Learning the 1-2-3 technique has helped me, leading to fewer tantrums in our household. I now have the courage of my convictions; when I decide to enforce a timeout for my children, I am able to remain calm and not have a parent tantrum myself!" The other benefits of attending the course is the realisation that many other parents have the same issues and it also helps to understand that some of the behaviours are just a phase and they will pass.

What changes have you noticed?

"I have found that understanding my children's behaviour has helped to switch off the stress of being a working mum. I feel more in control and my children are calmer as a result. Asking them how they feel and asking them for alternative solutions if they don't want to do something my way has led to the children suggesting different ways of doing things but achieving the same outcome. The result is that they are happier to have contributed to the problem solving and I as a parent get the outcome that I want!"

How has attending the course helped you support your children's learning?

"As a working mother in an organisation that is very driven, focused on tight timescales and high productivity, it is easy to slip into applying the same ethos at home. I've learnt that it is important to be their guide rather than their teacher, to nurture them like a flower, to really listen and let them lead, as they know their own capabilities. Recognising that they need their own downtime—that we don't have to fill their time with activities—they just need to chill out and do nothing sometimes."

"Being aware that they don't need to hit the same milestones as other children and that if they aren't keeping up, finding a way to re-phrase in a positive way, their achievements. Helping them understand the consequences of their actions—but in a positive way as much as possible, by giving them incentives for good behaviour."

What are the benefits for the corporation?

"I feel that my employer values me by providing this course for me. If I am able to have a less stressful time as a parent at home, then I am able to bring myself to work more focused and, as a consequence, be more productive." This means that the organisation is likely to experience higher retention rates for working parents, more employee engagement, and higher productivity.

### Case Study: Alex

Alex is a mother of two children (aged seven and three).

What were the challenges you were facing before attending "Coaching Skills for Parents" and how did you deal with them subsequently?

Alex attended the course to try to improve her parenting skills. She wanted more co-operation in the house and felt she was not getting the results that she wanted. She had received a strict upbringing, and wanted to know what other options there were.

What have been the key benefits of attending "Coaching Skills for Parents"?

Her children definitely noticed the changes in her. The course showed her that if she demonstrated empathy and patience, she would get better results. "So I now really empathise with my children, I understand if it is a big deal for them. I really listen—I ask them "how could you handle it better?" (whatever the problem is). In the past, I would not have known to acknowledge their feelings and been more inclined to tell them to "pull themselves together!" As a consequence, the children are much more co-operative. "They know that I am on their side now!" She also holds family meetings to talk about what is important and ask "what support do we all need?"

What changes have you noticed?

"I am much more patient and my children are now very confident about expressing their values and views because they are comfortable that they will get a good reaction from me. I realise that they are more capable than I gave them credit for in the past, and I let them take more responsibility. Consequently, they take on responsibility more easily. Since my break-up with my husband, my daughter assumes responsibility for putting my son to bed sometimes, or cleans the dishes for me without being asked."

She observed that the family meetings mean that the children have a real sense that they are part of a core unit as a family, as they are included in the decision making.

How has attending the course helped you support your children's learning?

"The course has helped me understand that every child is different. I now allow my daughter to take responsibility for when she does her homework and have found that she will often do it on Friday without prompting because she wants to spend time with us at the weekend.

Whereas before, I would make it my responsibility! I also used to work with her when she was doing her homework, which she didn't like. I now let her be independent and have a go first and then I review it with her. One of the things that the course stamped on my mind is that there is not one formula for all children." She constantly refers to the Parent Coaching Workbook: "It is my bible for life; as things happen in the family, I refer to it a lot."

## Putting it into practice in schools and organisations

In the UK, the Children Act 2004 established a duty on local authorities to ensure co-operation between agencies and a duty on key partners, including education, to co-operate (Arthur, Grainger, & Wray, 2006). This strategy led to a cluster of schools in London, consisting of seven primary schools, one children's centre, and two secondary schools, committing to running coaching courses for the parents at their schools.

*Every Child Matters: The Next Steps* (DfES 2004, in Arthur, Grainger, & Wray, 2006) set out the five outcomes (for children) that shaped the *Change for Children Agenda*. Within each outcome, it also stated how parents can contribute to achieving the outcome:

- be healthy: parents, carers, and families promote healthy choices;
- stay safe: parents, carers, and families provide safe homes and stability;
- enjoy and achieve: parents, carers, and families support learning;
- make a positive contribution: parents, carers, and families promote positive behaviour;
- achieve economic wellbeing: parents, carers, and families are supported to be economically active.

"Coaching for Parents" particularly connects with the need to make a positive contribution, since it encourages parents to promote positive behaviour. The course also links in with the need to enjoy and achieve, since it empowers parents to support the learning of their children through awareness of children's needs. This is evident in the feedback we received from parents who attended the courses and in the case studies mentioned earlier.

According to Arthur and colleagues (2006), *Every Child Matters* has contributed to shifting the system of children's services from intervention to prevention, with services working together more effectively. The idea of prevention links well with the foundation of "Coaching Skills for Parents", which is about giving parents encouragement, tools, and the understanding they need to empower them as parents and take responsibility for themselves and their children. We aim to create independence and demonstrate unconditional positive regard for the parents. Specifically, we are not trying to "fix" anything, as their parenting is not considered to be broken in the first place.

The outcomes included in *Every Child Matters* are designed to both protect children and maximise their potential. The overall aim is to reduce the number of children who experience educational failure, engage in offending and anti-social behaviour, suffer from ill health, or become teenage parents (DfES, 2003, cited in Arthur, Grainger, & Wray, 2006). With regard to "Coaching Skills for Parents", most of our participants have said that they feel more able to support their children's learning having taken part in the course. Within *Every Child Matters*, there is an emphasis on the interdependence of family, school, and community strategies for improved educational outcomes for individual learners.

## Conclusion

Coaching for parents can have a significant positive impact on the relationship between parents and children. When coaching helps parents to improve the way they communicate with their children, children are likely to enjoy learning more, both at home and at school. The results of the parent coaching link directly to the five *Every Child Matters* outcomes and are, therefore, a very useful tool for local authorities, schools, and educational organisations to adopt.

Coaching for parents can positively affect the lives of children across all walks of life, as illustrated in our case studies. It can also be introduced to a wider audience of parents by delivering it to workplaces in all sectors, driven by the need to improve retention rates for employees (who are parents), as part of a diversity or corporate social responsibility agenda, to increase employee engagement and satisfaction.

# References

Arthur, J., Grainger, T., & Wray, D. (2006). *Learning to Teach in the Primary School*. London: Routledge.

Berk, L. (2008), *Child Development* (8th edn). Needham Heights, MA: Allyn & Bacon.

Biddulph, S. (1998). *The Secret of Happy Children*. London: HarperCollins.

Bruner, J. (1960). *The Process of Education*. Cambridge, MA: Harvard University Press.

Faber, A., & Mazlish, E. (2001). *How to Talk So Kids Will Listen, and Listen So Kids Will Talk*. London: Piccadilly Press.

Freedman, J. L. (1965). Long-term behavioural effects of cognitive dissonance. *Journal of Experimental Social Psychology*, 1: 145–155.

Golawski, A. (2004). Towards the development of an NLP model for coaching. Unpublished dissertation: Henley Management College.

Grant, A. M., Passmore, J., Cavanagh, M., & Parker, H. (2010). The state of play in coaching. *International Review of Industrial & Organizational Psychology*, 25: 125–168.

Guldberg, H. (2009). *Reclaiming Childhood. Freedom and Play in an Age of Fear*. London: Routledge.

Hart, B., & Risley, T. (1995). *Meaningful Differences in the Everyday Experience of Young American Children*. Baltimore, MD: Brookes.

Hartley-Brewer, E. (2005). *Raising and Praising Boys*. London: Vermilion.

Holt, J. (1991). *How Children Learn*. London: Penguin.

Kline, N. (1998). *Time to Think: Listening to Ignite the Human Mind*. London: Cassell.

Layard, R., & Dunn, J. (2009). *A Good Childhood*. London: Penguin.

Lucas, B. (2006). *Happy Families: How to Make One, How to Keep One*. London: BBC Active.

Matheson, D. (2004). *An Introduction to the Study of Education* (2nd edn). London: David Fulton.

Mueller, C. M., & Dweck, C. S. (1998). Praise for intelligence can undermine children's motivation and performance. *Journal of Personality and Social Psychology*, 75: 33–52.

Palmer, S. (2006). *Toxic Childhood. How the Modern World is Damaging Our Children and What We Can Do about It*. London: Orion.

Rosenthal, R., & Jacobson, L. (1968). *Pygmalion in the Classroom*. New York: Holt, Rinehart and Winston.

Salmon, P. (1995). *Psychology in the Classroom*. London: Cassell.

Santrock, J. (2004). *Child Development*. New York: McGraw-Hill.

Skynner, R., & Cleese, J. (1997). *Families and How to Survive Them*. London: Vermilion.

Starr, J. (2008). *Brilliant Coaching; How to Be a Brilliant Coach in the Workplace*. Harlow: Pearson.

Steiner, R. (1996). *The Education of the Child and Early Lectures on Education*. Massachusetts: Anthroposophic Press.

Thomas, L. (2005). *The 7-Day Parent Coach*. London: Random House.

*Time Use Survey* (2006). London: Office of National Statistics.

Wearmouth, J. (2000). *Special Educational Provision: Meeting the Challenges in Schools*. London: Hodder & Stoughton

Wilson, A. (2011). *How to Be a Parent Champion and Add Magic to Your Family*. Maidstone: Every Family Matters.

Wiseman, R. (2009). *59 Seconds: Think a Little, Change a Lot*. London: Macmillan.

Websites:

www.nineteenminutes.com

www.parentgym.com

# CHAPTER NINE

# Creating coaching cultures for learning

*Christian van Nieuwerburgh and Jonathan Passmore*

## Introduction

As we have shown throughout this book, coaching has a unique contribution to make in educational settings and allows powerful learning to occur in carefully constructed environments. This chapter considers how to re-create, in schools and other learning organisations, the conditions in which coaching can be effective. In other words, how can we create "coaching cultures for learning"?

As the focal point of the communities of which they are a part, schools are the ideal context in which to grow coaching cultures for learning. As we have shown already, there is a considerable and growing body of evidence that coaching improves results for individuals and organisations. More specifically, the UK's National College for School Leadership (NCSL) concludes that "there is strong evidence that coaching promotes learning and builds capacity for change in schools" (Creasy & Paterson, 2005). It follows, therefore, that successful implementation of coaching cultures within schools (based on proven coaching principles) can lead to improved environments for learning. This, in turn, will mean better results for students, staff, and the wider community.

It is important for us, at this point, to reconnect with the real purpose of schools. Jim Collins, a leading American business thinker, states unequivocally that "we must reject the idea—well-intentioned, but dead wrong—that the primary path to greatness in the social sectors is to become 'more like a business'" (Collins, 2006, p. 1). While schools have sizeable budgets that they manage and many now employ business managers and business directors, we must be careful to remember that they are *not* commercial businesses. Collins suggests that in the public sector, the question should not be " 'How much money do we make . . .' but 'How effectively do we deliver on our mission and make a distinctive impact, relative to our resources?' " (ibid. , p. 5). We would argue that this applies to all educational organisations, regardless of whether they are in the public or private sector. Fundamentally, well-led schools, colleges, and universities should necessarily focus on the outcomes for their students, and not solely on financial indicators. The key question for educators, then, is: "How much of an impact are we making on the children, young people, or learners in this organisation, within the limits of our resources?" If this is the case, the aims of educational organisations and of coaching are the same: to support people to achieve more of their potential.

So, what might this look like for a school at the embedded stage of developing their coaching culture? Hayes Park Primary School in the UK was identified by NCSL as having a well-established culture of coaching (see Chapter Ten). Its senior coach believes that coaching works best when the coach

- is very focused and is able to relate continually each stage of the activity back to the learner's goal'
- is a good listener and can pick up the nuances of the learner's talk;
- is patient and a good judge of when to ask a question and how to ask it;
- can formulate questions in response to the discussion with the learner;
- can rephrase questions and prompts when there is a silence;
- avoids putting forward answers;
- avoids preset questions. (Creasy & Paterson, 2005)

## *Essential elements of a coaching culture for learning*

So, what are the essential elements of successful coaching practice and how can we transfer these into learning organisations? In Table 9.1, we consider some generally agreed characteristics of effective coaching relationships.

Combining the characteristics described in Table 9.1 creates a unique environment for individuals to engage in powerful and meaningful conversations. The learning that takes place often leads to better

*Table 9.1.* Characteristics of effective coaching.

| Characteristic | Description |
| --- | --- |
| Mutual trust | Trust is the cornerstone of a successful coaching partnership. Some of this trust is created through the confidential nature of coaching. The rest is built through the relationship and over time. |
| Timeliness | The fact that coaching takes place regularly, dealing with issues that are current and relevant for the coachee means that the intervention is "just-in-time". This is not the case with many "one-off" professional development opportunities currently available to educational staff. |
| Awareness of the need for change | Often, coachees are aware of the need for change when entering into coaching relationships. This awareness is critical if the coachee is to take positive steps towards better outcomes. In other words, it is important for the coaching opportunity to be voluntary. |
| Ownership of goals | The most successful coachees identify their own goals and related tasks through the coaching relationship. Goals and targets are not imposed from external sources. |
| Supportive relationships | Coaches are always present in a supportive capacity (even when asking challenging questions) to help the coachee to achieve more of their potential. Coaching should provide a motivational and encouraging context for the coachee. |
| Genuine care | For successful outcomes, coaches need to demonstrate respect and genuine care for the coachee and their goals. |
| Positive outlook | Good coaches are always forward-looking and optimistic, seeking out what is positive in their coachees. |

outcomes for coachees and raises their levels of self-esteem and motivation. Bresser and Wilson identify some other commonly mentioned benefits: "enhanced personal and organizational performance, better work–life balance, higher motivation, better self-reflection, optimized decision making and improved change management" (2006, p. 11).

By recreating the characteristics of effective coaching conversations in educational organisations, there will be an increased likelihood of emotionally intelligent leaders working with valued and motivated staff in positive and healthy learning environments. Students would thrive in an organisation that models a supportive and ambitious learning community. Most importantly, the supportive environment would encourage everyone to seek out more of their (sometimes hidden) potential.

## Steps towards a coaching culture for learning

If we accept that coaching cultures can enhance learning experiences, how can we start to move towards creating them? Three approaches are discussed here and they might be helpful in understanding the process. Each brings a slightly different perspective and we invite you to consider where you would locate your organisation in its journey towards a coaching culture (see "Reflection exercise", below).

## Creating a coaching culture: the competence model

One way of understanding the steps towards a coaching culture is based on a well-known learning model probably developed by psychologist Noel Burch in the early 1970s (Adams, see: www.gordon-training.com).

### Unconscious incompetence

This is the stage where there is little or no awareness of the benefits of a coaching culture. There is no shared understanding of the term "coaching", and many people will say or think that they are "too busy" to get engaged with coaching, which is considered to be of limited value.

---

**Reflection exercise**

*Where are we now?*

Just as every coachee is unique, so, too, is every organisation. You might already be leading or working for a supportive learning organisation that fully embraces the concept of a coaching culture for learning. Or else your organisation might just be at the very early stages of thinking about the possible benefits of coaching. Or, more likely, it is somewhere in between.

According to Erik de Haan, "coaching is predominantly an exercise in *self-understanding* and *self-changing* on the part of the coachee" (de Haan, 2009, p. 52). Similarly, creating a coaching culture for learning is all about *organisational self-awareness*. It is an important first step to know (as an organisation) where you are. Equally important is the notion that the development of a coaching culture for learning is *self-directed*. Even if there is a need to involve third parties in a change programme, ownership of the process must rest with the organisation and the people within it.

As you read about the three approaches to understanding the process of creating a coaching culture, please reflect on your organisation's place within each.

---

## Conscious incompetence

At this stage, there is a general recognition that some change is needed in the school: a new way of thinking, a more dynamic culture or a "turn-around". Coaching might be discussed as one way of moving forward, although the term itself might be confused with mentoring or counselling. A few influential people might be prepared to explore the idea of coaching further while others are doubtful or cynical.

## Conscious competence

This is a critically important stage. Coaching will be better understood and have some key champions within the organisation. Coaching is broadly accepted as a positive intervention that will allow the organisation and individuals within it to achieve better results. Much learning is still taking place, and along with successes there might be difficulties. It is important in this phase to be resilient, working hard to ensure that a coaching culture for learning becomes embedded in the organisation.

*Unconscious competence*

This is an ideal place to be. The coaching culture will be embedded and well understood by all members of the organisation. It becomes the normal way of being as the organisation continues to develop organically. It is no longer a "coaching initiative" or "programme", but a natural way of being.

## Creating a coaching culture: stages

We will now consider an alternative four-stage process developed by Clutterbuck and Megginson (2005). This approach relates directly to coaching and has been used in a number of organisations as a way of creating a coaching culture. Clutterbuck and Megginson describe the following four stages.

> Nascent: at this stage, the organisation "shows little or no commitment to creating a coaching culture" (p. 96). Coaching activity is sporadic and unco-ordinated.
> Tactical: at this stage, the organisation might have "recognised the value of establishing a coaching culture, but there is little understanding of what that means" (ibid.).
> Strategic: at this stage, the organisation will have invested considerable resources into educating staff about the value of coaching as well as training. "Top management have accepted the need to demonstrate good practice" (ibid.). Leaders connect strategic business drivers with coaching initiatives.
> Embedded: at this (ideal) stage, "people at all levels are engaged in coaching" (p. 97) and "coaching and mentoring are so seamlessly built into the structure of HR systems that they occur automatically" (ibid.) As a result, the organisation can tackle difficult issues and focus on improvement.

## Creating a coaching culture: journey

A third model of stages towards creating a coaching culture presents the various stages as part of a "journey" (Passmore & Jastrzebska,

2011). This journey has five staging posts from the use of external coaching practitioners to using coaching across the wider network with all stakeholders, including governors, parents, and partners. This is summarised in Figure 9.1.

We propose that it is important to start by defining a coaching culture. The term itself is widely misused and often has been taken to mean simply that coaching is used widely with teachers or with students. However, for this to be part of a coaching culture for learning, we believe it should be used consistently across the wider school community.

We define a coaching culture for learning as one where coaching, the use of reflective and provocative questions, is used consistently by all partners across the school community, to help develop learning, understanding and personal responsibility in others from staff, to parents and from students to governors and wider stakeholders.

## Stage one: informal external coaches

Many learning institutions hold the presumption that if they use external coaches they already have a coaching culture. However, from

*Figure 9.1.*    Five levels on the journey to a coaching culture.

our experience of working with many different schools, the appointment of a coach to work with the head teacher or deputy head teacher is helpful, but this does not necessarily lead to a shift in the organisational culture. Coaching needs to extend beyond the leadership team and across the organisation. It needs to be planned and be part of a wider process to drive change and transform the way the school or college works and learns.

*Stage two: strategic use of external coaching*

At stage two on the journey towards a coaching culture for learning, we would suggest that coaches would be appointed in a professional manner, and in a way where there is a plan for how the external coaches can share their knowledge so that the senior team both learn the coaching way of developing others and start to use it consistently with the staff, and second, their own coaching is tied to a set of objectives for the school and specifically links to the organisation's development plans.

*Stage three: coaching as a management style*

The third stage of building a coaching culture for learning involves the move to introduce coaching for all staff, not only the senior or middle managers. At this stage, schools have tended to move towards creating a cadre of internal coaches, as the use of external coaches for all staff is expensive and unaffordable for most schools.

The first step in this process is building a pool of internal coaches. This involves selecting and training individuals throughout the organisation. From experience, we have found that inviting volunteers is helpful, as such individuals are more likely to remain involved with the future programme and make time for coachees than those pressed into coaching service. Ultimately, this should mean that all staff being trained in coaching skills are able to use coaching in multiple interactions with others, helping each other to learn through, when appropriate, useful, open, and reflective questions.

*Stage four: coaching for all*

The fourth stage for organisations on the journey to creating a coaching culture for learning is to extend coaching from management discussion into learning discussions with students. Teachers can use coaching as a way of encouraging learning in the classroom, alongside tried and tested didactic methods. This involves asking provocative questions, encouraging students to think and discover the answers to questions for themselves.

### Stage five: coaching across the school network

The fifth stage is spreading coaching beyond the traditional boundary of schools and communities, into the wider community. This involves the use of coaching in conversations with parents, with governors, with stakeholders, and encouraging each of these groups to learn about coaching and to use coaching with their children and others in appropriate ways which maximise learning and facilitate the development of personal responsibility.

---

Activity

Once you have decided where you would place your organisation in any or all of the three approaches described above, ask yourself this question: "What would other people in my organisation say?" Think of a few members of staff from across the organisation. As a next step, why not ask them?

---

### Working towards a coaching culture for learning

How well are you doing currently? You may like to take a few minutes to complete Table 9.2. Be as honest as you can.

Completing this table will give you a good indication of your own perceptions about how well your organisation is doing currently as a coaching culture for learning. Where you have rated yourself highly, it is important to recognise the strengths in your organisation and look for opportunities to both celebrate and promote those aspects. Where you have given yourself a lower rating, that could be an area that the organisation chooses to prioritise for development.

*Table 9.2.*   Self-assessment.

| Elements of a coaching culture for learning | How it might be represented in a school or college | Your assessment 0: No, not at all 10: Yes, all the time |
|---|---|---|
| Mutual trust | Staff and students trust one another | |
| Timeliness | All staff and students have opportunities to discuss any learning or development issue at any time | |
| Awareness of the need for change | Staff and students want things to be better, are open to new ideas and looking for ways of developing themselves and the organisation | |
| Ownership of goals | Staff and students play a significant role in setting and achieving their own goals | |
| Supportive relationships | Staff and students support one another through praise and encouragement | |
| Genuine care | Staff and students show respect and genuine care for one another | |
| Positive outlook | Staff and students are positive about each other and the school | |

## Using appreciative inquiry to embed a coaching culture for learning

Coaches use a number of theoretical and organisational development tools during their coaching conversations. Appreciative inquiry (AI) is an area of work that has been developed by David Cooperrider and Suresh Srivastra (Whitney & Trosten-Bloom, 2003). It has been applied in a variety of contexts and is now a popular model for both the commercial and public sectors (Lewis, Passmore, & Cantore, 2011). Its principle is to focus on an organisation's strengths and to build on these, rather than to focus on areas of perceived "weakness", which can lead to negativity and lack of motivation.

Our view is that educational improvement has focused too closely on a deficit model. In situations where improvement is necessary, identifying, analysing, and scrutinising the institution's weaknesses often exacerbates some of the problems that the organisation is facing, increases stress for key leadership team members, and demoralises both staff and students.

Below, we have proposed one way of using an appreciative approach to start to work towards a coaching culture for learning. As stated earlier in this book, there are no blueprints for embedding coaching in educational organisations. In addition, it is important to recognise that such transformations require commitment, time, and energy. The proposed approach set out in Table 9.3, therefore, is very open to adaptation and development.

*Pre-work: setting the scene*

By its very nature, it is impossible to "implement" a coaching culture for learning just as it would be counterproductive to impose a confidential, safe relationship on an unsuspecting coachee! As with coaching, the essential element of mutual trust is nurtured through the joint creation of a safe learning environment. So, the very first step is to involve others. It is impossible to build a positive learning culture alone.

Before the work of co-creating a coaching culture for learning can begin, the concept of coaching will need to be discussed openly and honestly. For obvious reasons, those starting to share their thoughts about coaching will want to model best practice, either by undertaking

*Table 9.3.*    Stages of an appreciative approach towards a coaching culture for learning.

| Stages | Who needs to be involved? |
| --- | --- |
| Pre-work: discussion and planning | School leadership team |
| Discovery stage | School leadership team |
| Discovery stage | Whole school workforce and students |
| Dreaming stage | Whole school workforce and students |
| Designing stage | Whole school workforce and students |
| Destiny stage | Whole school workforce and students |
| Continuing work: encouragement | School leadership team |

some professional development around coaching or by having a coach themselves. Where schools in the UK have successfully introduced coaching cultures, an important prerequisite has been the commitment and "buy-in" from members of a school's leadership team. From that point of view, it is important to create opportunities within leadership team meetings to start talking about the potential benefits of a coaching culture for learning. As part of the groundwork, we would recommend that a school leadership team should complete the "discovery stage" of the AI task for themselves before involving the whole school workforce.

The first part of building a coaching culture is to *engage* people in your organisation with the concept of a coaching culture for learning. Building a positive learning culture together is an essential part of the process. People will need an opportunity to explore what they want for themselves and the organisation. In this stage, it is important to involve as many stakeholders as possible.

| 1 | Appreciative Inquiry: Discovery Stage<br><br>*"What's good about the way we work together already?"*<br><br>What are we best at?<br>What is behind our success?<br>What motivates us?<br>What are we all about? |
|---|---|

As mentioned above, we would recommend that the leadership team spend some time with the questions of the discovery stage before involving the rest of the school community. Rather than scheduling additional meetings, perhaps this could be introduced into an exisiting meetings structure. Commitment and enthusiasm from the leaders of an organisation is a necessary prerequisite for the co-creation of a successful coaching culture for learning.

Once the leadership team has had sufficient opportunity to start thinking about the strengths and successes of the current team, this stage will need to be repeated with the whole-school workforce. In an ideal setting, students should be involved in this process as well (perhaps during an assembly, or in smaller groups or classes). After introducing the concept of a coaching culture for learning, it will be important to create opportunities for staff and students to talk about what is already good about working in the organisation. What dreams or ambitions do they have for themselves and the organisation? What deeper moral purpose drives them? If all of this is implicit in your organisation, make it explicit. Our dreams, our moral purpose, and the things we are passionate about are the most potent motivators. Made explicit, the school's moral purpose will re-energise members of staff and bring them together. At the same time, students will have an opportunity to focus on what is good about their school. Crucially, the shared purpose is the reason for working together to improve the way in which people learn together in the organisation.

*Sample activities*

1.   Positive perceptual positions: relationships within the school
     - Divide people into three (or six) groups.
     - Each group is given the task of discussing how others might perceive relationships within the school.
     - Each group (or two groups) is assigned "student", "parent", "visitor".
     - Groups then discuss the question of "What is good about how staff work together?" from the point of view that they have been assigned.
     - Groups should capture the perceptions, along with "evidence" (i.e., what the student/parent/visitor would actually see that would lead them to their perception).
     - Each group then presents their information to the other groups.

2.   Current reality and desired future
     - Ask groups to draw a star as their "desired future" in the top right of a sheet of paper. In the bottom left, ask them to write "here and now" (Figure 9.2).
     - In groups, staff or students should decide what is positive about the way they already work or learn together.
     - Everyone should be given an opportunity to contribute at least one positive aspect.

Here and now

*Figure 9.2.* Current reality and desired future.

- When groups have jotted down all the existing attributes, ask them to identify the three most important things. In other words, "What do you think must be protected at all costs?"
- Ask them not to write anything in the "desired future" yet.
- Once groups have completed this task, they share their three most important things with the other groups. Groups should be given an opportunity to explain any challenges or difficulties they encountered with the task.
- A facilitator should aim to capture the "three most important things" of every group on a flipchart or board.

3.  Agreed moral purpose
    - Divide the group between tables. Allow five minutes for each person, in silence, to draft a one-sentence description of the organisation's moral purpose. How would they describe, in one sentence, the fundamental purpose of their organisation?
    - Allow another 10–20 minutes for the groups on tables to agree one sentence. They will need to hear everyone's sentences, and then negotiate it down to one sentence that everyone can agree to.
    - Finally, ask the groups to choose two words from their sentence that they would be prepared to fight for.
    - The facilitator then captures the two words from each table, and then asks the groups to combine all the words into one statement.

| 2 | Appreciative Inquiry: Dreaming Stage |
|---|---|
| | *"What might happen?"* |
| | What can we achieve together (as a learning organisation)? |
| | What outcomes would make us proud? |

The next stage is to explore the possibilities. This is the opportunity for people to dream. What could the educational organisation achieve for its students? What are their individual ambitions, and those of the organisation? In coaching, the exploration of possibilities and the opportunity for coachees to share their dreams add real energy to conversations. A well-expressed dream or ambition is a powerful motivator for the coachee, who often needs to change his or her own behaviour or work harder to achieve the goals. For an educational organisation, it is important that members of staff and students can agree on an aspiration or motivational goal that makes the required additional effort worthwhile.

*Sample activities*

Activities should focus on exploring shared ambitions and aspirations. This stage creates opportunities for participants to declare what is important to them. This stage can also confirm that some of the deeper motivators are shared.

4.  Sharing dreams
    - Complete the "desired future" star on the "Current reality and desired future diagram (Figure 9.2).
    - On tables, groups are given fifteen minutes to discuss a motivational ambition or goal that everyone on the table can agree with.
    - These "dreams" are shared and captured on a flipchart.
    - The facilitator leads a discussion on similarities first and then any significant differences.
    - As a conclusion, the facilitator points out that the creation of a coaching culture for learning will support them in achieving their ambitions.

5.  No constraints
    - On tables, groups brainstorm the question "If we could do anything as an organisation, what would we do?"
    - Groups can be as creative or as imaginative as they want to be.
    - The scribe or artist captures the ideas or image that has been agreed.
    - These are shared among the group.

- The facilitator then leads a discussion on what is achievable, using the ideas and images as an indication of what members of the groups are passionate about.

| 3 | Appreciative Inquiry: Designing Stage |
|---|---|
| | *"How will a coaching culture for learning look and feel?"* |
| | What will we look forward to (as a learning organisation)? |
| | What can we start doing now? |

*How will we make it happen?*

Once participants have had a genuine and thoughtful opportunity to dream about the possibilities, it is time to start working towards the practical steps that will take the organisation in the right direction. With a shared understanding of the organisation's current strengths and a clearer notion of what is important, it will be possible to start planning with real energy and purpose. The co-creation of a coaching culture for learning will be a firm foundation for a successful, constantly improving educational organisation.

*Sample activities*

Activities should focus on identifying what each element of the coaching culture will mean in a specific organisation.

6.   Coaching culture for learning in practice
- Using Table 9.4 as a prompt, ask participants (in groups) to complete the "in practice" column.
- Coaching triads can be used to explore some of these elements further. Ask the group to split into triads.
- Each member of a triad is asked to select one element of the Coaching Culture for Learning. The members rotate in the following roles: coach, coachee and note-taker.
- The coach asks the coachee open questions about how each element can be put into practice in their organisation.
   "How will this element be visible in our organisation?"
   "What real difference will it make on a day-to-day basis?"

*Table 9.4.*   Creating a coaching culture for learning.

| Elements of a coaching culture for learning | In practice | What success might look like |
|---|---|---|
| Mutual trust | | |
| Timeliness | | |
| Awareness of the need for change | | |
| Ownership of goals | | |
| Supportive relationships | | |
| Genuine care | | |
| Positive outlook | | |

"How will it make a difference for staff/children and young people/parents?"

● To allow the coachee quality thinking and speaking time, the note-taker should make brief notes to capture the main points of the discussion. These notes will be used to complete the "in practice" column.

● Each group is asked to complete the table.

● Each group is then given one or two of the elements to collate. In their groups, team members are asked to collate all the suggestions for the elements they have been assigned. For example, one group would receive all the completed rows for "Mutual trust" and "Timeliness". The group would work together to combine all the suggested responses.

● After the session, all the collated responses are copied on one table (Table 9.4).

| 4 | Appreciative Inquiry: Destiny Stage |
|---|---|
| | *"How will you feel when we have achieved it?"* |
| | How will we be feeling? |
| | What will members of the community be saying about the organisation? |

*How will we know it is happening?*

To ensure that progress can be monitored and achievements celebrated, it is important at the outset to define success. What will people be hearing, seeing, feeling, or saying when the organisation has a coaching culture for learning?

### Sample activities

Activities should focus on discussing and agreeing success criteria. This should be followed by an action planning stage.

For the purposes of measuring progress, it is important to agree on success criteria so that achievements can be celebrated. Table 9.5 can be used to fill in the final column: "What success might look like".

7.   Imagining success
   ● Each group is given one element to discuss. They will have the "element" and a description of what this means in practice in their organisation.
   ● The group is then asked to complete the final column by answering the question: "What will be different when the organisation embraces a coaching culture for learning?" It is important for this to be described in a way that will be easily observable.

8.   Action planning
   ● Once the above activity is completed, elements are passed around so that the groups are working on another element.
   ● Each group should discuss an action plan for moving toward the successful outcome. The question for brainstorming is "What can we do now to move closer to the outcome we want?"
   ● Proposed actions are submitted to the leadership team, who will consider and incorporate suggestions into the organisational development plan.

### Continuing work

As the organisation starts to work towards its aspirations, an important part of ensuring success and continued commitment is for everyone involved to experience and celebrate change. Change will be slow and sporadic unless a significant number of individuals choose to adopt new behaviours. The leadership team has five key responsibilities in this regard.

1.  Ensure suggestions and proposals for moving towards a coaching culture for learning are incorporated into the organisation's strategic plans.
2.  Model the required new behaviours and have a clear expectation that others will do the same.
3.  Encourage implementation of action plans while being available to support colleagues.
4.  Engage with challenges and difficulties quickly and effectively, seeing them as evidence that change is taking place and listening carefully to the concerns of members of the team.
5.  Celebrate successes and regularly reflect on what is going well.

## Successful outcomes

You will be able to achieve many successes by working collaboratively with a group of like-minded and positive colleagues. However, you will never "complete" the process of embracing a coaching culture. For one thing, at the heart of a coaching culture for learning is a desire to continuously improve and find better ways of achieving what is important. Equally, coaching is a powerful intervention because it is always forward looking. However good a particular coaching session is, it is never repeated. A good result in coaching simply leads to new opportunities and further successes. It is also useful to reflect on Collins' observations about greatness in relation to organisations:

> No matter how much you have achieved, *you will always be merely good relative to what you can become.* Greatness is an inherently dynamic process, not an end point. The moment you think of yourself as great, your slide towards mediocrity will have already begun. (2006, p. 9).

## Conclusions

Building a coaching culture in a school or college is a journey. Like most journeys, they usually start with a first step; introducing coaching for staff or into the classroom. Like most journeys, unplanned events occur, and we take a slightly longer route and learn from the experience. As you will see from the case studies in this book, organisations have approached coaching from different directions.

Practitioners, students, academics, and policy-makers in the UK, the USA, and Australia are embracing the role of coaching in education. We hope that what you have read will encourage you to do the same.

## References

Adams, L. (2012). Learning a new skill is easier said than done. www.gordontraining.com/free-workplace-articles/learning-a-new-skill-is-easier-said-than-done (accessed on 28 March 2012).

Bresser, F., & Wilson, C. (2006). What is coaching? In: J. Passmore (Ed.), *Excellence in Coaching: The Industry Guide* (pp. 9–25). London: Kogan Page.

Centre for the Use of Research and Evidence in Education (CUREE) (2005). *National Framework for Mentoring and Coaching*. London: DfES.

Clutterbuck, D., & Megginson, D. (2005). *Making Coaching Work: Creating a Coaching Culture*. London: CIPD.

Collins, J. (2006). *Good to Great and the Social Sectors*. London: Random House.

Creasy, J., & Paterson, F. (2005). *Leading Coaching in Schools*. Nottingham: NCSL.

de Haan, E. (2008). *Relational Coaching: Journeys towards Mastering One-to-One Learning*. Chichester: John Wiley.

Lewis, S., Passmore, J., & Cantore, S. (2011). *Appreciative Inquiry for Change Management: Using AI to Facilitate Organizational Development* (2nd edn). London: Kogan Page.

Passmore, J., & Jastrzebska, K. (2011). Building a coaching culture: a development journey for organisational development. *Coaching Review, 1*(3): 89–101.

Whitney, D., & Trosten-Bloom, A. (2003). *The Power of Appreciative Inquiry: A Practical Guide to Positive Change*. San Francisco, CA: Berrett-Koehler.

# PART II
# CASE STUDIES

# CHAPTER TEN

# Coaching in primary schools: a case study

*Neil Suggett*

## Introduction

Hayes Park is a West London primary school of 730 children and 100 staff and has become known as the "coaching school". The school has been judged as "outstanding" in the Ofsted Inspections in 2003 and 2007. In this chapter, I explain how coaching has become a fundamental part of how we do things and its impact on learning and leading. I also summarise how coaching is being used on a day-to-day basis and share some insights on the introduction of a coaching approach.

People have many different understandings of the term "coaching". Our working definition of coaching has been developed over the past eight years and reflects our collective learning about a coaching approach. The key elements are:

- coaching is a process that unlocks a person's potential in order to maximise performance, whether that be a child or an adult;
- coaching enables the individual to learn, rather than being the recipient of teaching;
- coaching takes an optimistic view of future possibilities and is not focused upon deficits or past failures;

- coaching is a flexible process that can be tailored to meet the needs of the individual learner, regardless of the learner's age.

The reason we have become passionate about coaching is very simple—it works! It works for both children and adults. Coaching is deeply embedded within our school culture and is our predominant leadership style. Other leadership styles are employed when appropriate, but a coaching approach is our default position. Our vision statement elaborates our desire to be an inclusive community of children and adults committed to learning excellence. Coaching addresses the individual or team goals and develops the individual or team in the process. The learning comes from the doing—a basic tenet of effective education.

A coaching approach to learning and leadership fits comfortably with a philosophy of shared responsibility. Indeed, coaching is a key component of shared leadership at Hayes Park. The reasons for sharing leadership are, in my view, self-evident, and are summarised in the following beliefs.

1.  Heroic leadership is not sustainable and really effective headship is about orchestrating the work of the other stakeholders in the organisation.
2.  Hierarchical leadership is hard to justify in a democratic environment, although in our current legal structure shared leadership cannot mean equal accountability.
3.  Shared leadership unleashes the power of collegiality and emphasises the importance of teamwork—together each achieves more.
4.  A team approach is inclusive and values the strengths and capabilities of each member.
5.  Shared leadership releases creativity and involves a balance of support and challenge.
6.  Sharing leadership generates alignment on vision and values because the stakeholders are involved in the construction process.

The genesis of our interest in coaching was stimulated by a chance conversation with our Investors in People (IIP) adviser in 2002. Having successfully achieved the standard as an IIP organisation, we were asking "where next?" Our IIP adviser suggested coaching was the way of the future and I enrolled on a coaching programme. The programme was a revelation to me. I now had the vocabulary and skills to develop a systematic approach to coaching. Intuitively, I had always believed in a person-centred approach to school leadership and management. The programme provided the underpinning theory and practice to develop a more coherent strategy.

The coach development programme lasted six months, and during this time I was required to coach colleagues inside my school and coachees from other disciplines. The power of the approach became immediately apparent to both coach and coachees. The lectures, the reading, and the practice provided me with the basic skills of coaching and an evangelistic zeal to share my newfound knowledge. Initially, I did this by developing a programme for local head teachers and deputy head teachers. The attendees were very positive about the skills they had developed and the application to their own schools.

A second course quickly followed, and Deb Barlow, the deputy head teacher of Hayes Park, was one of the delegates. Deb began working with a group of coachees at our school as part of the course programme, and the success of these coaching sessions was immediately apparent. The coachees also attested to the power of the process and this generated interest in other Hayes Park colleagues. One stunningly successful piece of coaching that Deb completed resulted in a changed approach to the provision for additional needs across the whole school and underscored the power of the approach.

Deb and I decided to run our first school-based coach development programme at Hayes Park in summer 2004. The time was opportune, people were beginning to talk about the power of coaching, and I had gained experience from running several programmes with colleagues across London. Teachers were invited to nominate themselves for the six half-day programme and the bar was set very high—the six half days were Saturday mornings or during the holidays. A very committed group of six delegates embarked on this first programme.

The basic structure of the programme was one session per month over six months. This allowed ample time between sessions for the delegates to undertake practice coaching sessions with other colleagues and to do some background reading. The format of the course reflected my learning from the course I had attended and the expanding number of courses I had facilitated. The six sessions were as follows.

## An introduction to coaching

The first morning set the scene, outlining the theoretical background and introducing delegates to the GROW model (Alexander, 2006). Colleagues identified the opportunity to observe a real coaching session as the most significant part of this session. "So the key is asking and not telling!" A rhythm to this and future sessions developed: theory, practice, and a review of the learning. Initially, the practice coaching sessions addressed real issues at our school and the potential of the programme gradually became apparent to both facilitators and delegates. The "homework" for the month was to undertake at least two coaching sessions with colleagues from our school.

## Key skills

The second training event emphasised the importance of listening, questioning, and promoting action. The morning started with a review of the practice coaching sessions delegates had undertaken over the past month. The recurring theme was how difficult it is to ask and not tell. As teachers, we do a lot of telling, and people had found it difficult to resist telling the coachee what to do, particularly when that is what the coachee was expecting! The focus on listening for understanding was very powerful, as both a key element of effective coaching and as an aspiration for us as a school. We purchased multiple copies of John Whitmore's *Coaching for Performance* (Whitmore, 2002) and colleagues read avidly the appendix on questioning. The homework after this session was to coach somebody outside education on a work-related topic.

## Leadership, management, and coaching

The feedback at the start of this session emphasised how much easier it is to coach people for whom you have no line-management responsibility. This significant learning point informed a later decision about how to structure team coaching. This third session unpicked the differences between leadership, management, and coaching, with an emphasis on the skills required to be effective in each of these disciplines. The power of a school-based programme was reinforced once again. This was not a theoretical discussion, but, rather, how we should do things in the future. Each morning had a time set aside for practical coaching in pairs and triads, with increasing levels of observer feedback and collective review. The task before the next session was to coach a pupil.

## Mentoring, coaching, and counselling

This half-day started with a review of the pupil coaching sessions and the feedback was very positive. Most people had chosen to address behavioural issues with the intention of encouraging a pupil to take responsibility for her or his own behaviour. This led into a review of our approaches to mentoring, coaching, and counselling and the skills that a teacher needs to be effective in these areas. The dangers of feeling out of your depth were highlighted, and what to do in such circumstances discussed. Once again, the power of the discussion resided in what we do now in our school and what we would do in the future. Three months into the programme, delegates were noticing a greater "naturalness" about their coaching and a much more relaxed approach to framing questions. The task before the next session was to coach a team.

## Team coaching

The review of the team coaching undertaken during the month suggested that people were pleasantly surprised by how well their sessions had gone. The challenges of using the GROW model with a team were explored, particularly the complexity of uncovering a shared reality about the current state of play. The bulk of the session was invested in practical team coaching with each delegate having an opportunity to coach the group on a real issue. By the end of the session, six real issues had been addressed and clear plans of action had been agreed. We became dimly aware of the potential power of team coaching in shaping the future of our school. However, the six delegates and two facilitators represented a small percentage of the people involved in our school. The task before the last session was to reflect on how we could harness the power of coaching in developing our school.

## The Hayes Park coaching strategy

The final session involved a celebration of our collective learning and discussions about how we could move forward as a school. The coaching practice involved both individual and team coaching and a number of recurring themes emerged.

- We needed to increase the number of potential coaches in the school and, therefore, another development programme was planned.
- The group of eight coaches were all teachers, middle and senior leaders, and this gave the initiative an exclusivity that was out of keeping with the collegial nature of coaching.
- The group of coaches in the school needed to be broadened and it was vital that the next cohort of coaches included associate staff and a wider mix of teachers.
- The eight people would all seek to use coaching in a natural way in their day-to-day work and behave as action researchers. The central question we were seeking to answer was "How can coaching add value to what we do?"

The first coach development programme coincided with the national and local workforce development agenda. As a school, we were planning the transition from posts of responsibility (management points) to teaching and learning responsibilities (TLRs). We were moving from eighteen posts of responsibility to twelve TLRs and reorganising our leadership structure around four core teams all focused on learning. The four core teams were:

- teaching for learning—the team dealing with futures curriculum development and the leadership of the specific curriculum areas;
- supporting learning—the team creating the conditions for learning by developing the environment and support structures to enable high quality teaching;
- learning for all—the team leading the work on additional needs, both special educational needs and gifted and talented, and leading on behaviour management;
- Extending learning—the team charged with the responsibility for developing the extended schools agenda, our before- and after-school provision, and actively engaging with our community.

The four core teams were established in autumn 2004 and each one was led by the head teacher, a deputy head teacher, or an assistant head teacher. It was also decided to appoint four senior associate staff positions designated as strand manager, one within each core team. These four colleagues were appointed at interview and became pivotal players in our new structure. The four strand managers were also invited to attend the next coach development programme. At the same time, a key decision was made to establish a TLR for coaching. This person would have responsibility for leading coaching across the whole school and would co-ordinate the work of the fledgling coaches. The appointment of the TLRs was achieved with remarkable speed and positive intent, not least in that twelve people applied for twelve posts. Sarah Parkinson, one of the first cohort trainees, was appointed TLR for coaching.

The second coach development programme started in January 2005 and involved a group of four associate staff and eight teachers. The programme was modified to include two half-days and four twilight sessions. The content reflected the learning that had taken place during and after the first coach development programme, and Sarah Parkinson joined as the new TLR for coaching. This was an exciting and vibrant group and the breadth of experience the associate staff colleagues brought to the programme deepened the learning. It also became apparent that their timetables were more flexible, and this created a much wider range of ways forward. Their work with children had a slightly different texture, and the strand manager for "learning for all" was quickly able to incorporate coaching into the work she was doing with challenging behaviour. This group and the new TLR generated a momentum for coaching, not least because they were coaching much larger numbers of children and adults across the school. The teachers also developed innovative ways of using the GROW model with children as young as six.

The final session of cohort two agreed that the time was right to organise a whole-school training day for all staff. We now had a group of twenty trained coaches, and the plan was that they should be a central part in delivering this highly significant learning experience. It was agreed to have a general introduction, and then allocate people to small groups to observe a real coaching session led by one of the trained coaches. This session was reviewed, and then all staff were invited to coach and be coached in triads. Sarah Parkinson, Deb

Barlow, and I approached the day with a mixture of excitement and trepidation and were delighted by the response from colleagues. A variety of emotions were apparent in the colleagues being introduced to coaching: a desire to understand the process, a commitment to "having a go", and a level of healthy scepticism.

The chronology of the next stage of development is difficult to track in a coherent way as several things were happening at the same time. Malcolm Gladwell, in his book *Outliers* (2009), describes how successful initiatives often reflect a level of serendipity and opportunism. Upon reflection, both of these factors were apparent in the next stages of the development of coaching at Hayes Park. Retrospective description tends to make the process seem neater than it actually was. It would seem that a number of planned and unplanned occurrences built the momentum for coaching in our school. I have sought to capture these in the following list:

- a newly appointed and dynamic TLR for coaching;
- a leadership team committed to exploring the power of a coaching approach;
- the new opportunities created for both teaching and associate staff by the workforce development agenda;
- an "outstanding" Ofsted inspection in 2003 that had included the imperative to innovate and take risks;
- a group of newly appointed strand managers who were widely respected and brought a new dimension to school leadership;
- a growing external interest in the success of our coaching initiatives and the external validation of our work by local authority staff, Investors in People assessors, National College for School Leadership, and university students.

The increasing number of visitors, and, particularly, an MA student researching the impact of coaching as her dissertation topic, caused us to reflect and seek to measure the impact of coaching and its value for money. Billy Connolly famously once said, "I enjoy being interviewed as people ask me excellent questions and I find out what I am really thinking." This was certainly our experience! One particular seminal moment was marked by a two-day visit by Jim Wallace, a colleague from Scotland, who had been charged with the responsibility of setting up a coaching network in his local authority. He asked deep and searching questions, interviewed samples of staff and pupils, and provided a summary of the current state of play as he perceived it. He identified a number of key elements in the gathering momentum of coaching at Hayes Park.

1. The creation of a coaching room that provided a focal point for staff and pupils. The room had been an old chair store that was refurbished and set up with new furniture to facilitate the coaching process. The significance of this room had largely escaped us, although we were pleased with the opportunities it provided. Pupil guides showing visitors around the school explained the purpose and impact of the coaching room with economy and enthusiasm.

2. Separate interviews with different stakeholders in the school provided the opportunity to triangulate our thinking. The TLR for coaching handled the visit very successfully and, in the course of the dialogue with our visitor, refined her thinking and planning. A neutral, external researcher provided the opportunity for interviewees to be honest about the impact of coaching and to develop their own reflections.

3. This and other visits added to our collective self-esteem and the sense that we were developing something special that interested other educationalists.

4. We all learnt something from the visit, and the report provided a springboard for the next stage of development.

The development of coaching featured in our annual school improvement plans from 2004 onwards, and the increasing number of visitors and researchers (not least a researcher from CUREE developing the national framework for coaching and mentoring) caused us to refine the philosophy that underpinned our approach to coaching. We agreed the key elements and summarised them in the following list in 2005. At Hayes Park, we believe coaching

- should be a non-directive process;
- should be coachee-driven, s/he chooses the agenda;
- should be goal-centred and have an action outcome;
- should focus on the present and the future and not the past;
- should be an investment in our people.

A third cohort of coaches was established, with a time allocation of fifteen hours: six two-hour twilight sessions and three hours of inter-sessional tasks. The facilitating team was now much more experienced and all the delegates had experience of being coached. The programme had been modified, but contained the same basic elements. The team coaching session once again demonstrated the power of the approach and it was proposed by the delegates that a section of each training day should be set aside for team coaching with a neutral coach from another part of the school. This was adopted and has been in place ever since.

In the summer of 2006, we commissioned Vivienne Porritt from the London Institute of Education to evaluate the impact of coaching at our school. She highlighted the main strengths as

- the development of leadership skills at all levels;
- the quality of team relationships;
- the development of a solution focused approach;
- the quality of relationships between teaching and support staff;
- the support for individual pupils;
- the sense of being valued.

The next steps suggested were as follows.

1. Developing a coaching approach to learning with individual and targeted groups of pupils.
2. Using a coaching approach with whole classes, for example in Assessment for Learning.
3. Older pupils or peers acting as coaches to other children with the focus on learning issues.
4. The alignment of continuing professional development (CPD), performance management and coaching.
5. Coaching support for governors.

All of the next steps were addressed with alacrity over the next academic year, with the exception of proposal 5 (coaching support for governors). In a fairly arbitrary way, coaching was subdivided into *coaching for development* (the initiatives with adults) and *coaching for learning* (the initiatives with children).

The coaching for development strand was already well established. A number of approaches to structuring individual coaching had been piloted, such as an allocated coach or a duty coach, and it was now agreed policy that individual coaching should be an entitlement, available upon request. The request could be made by a coachee for a named coach, or an offer could be made by a line manager. The strand manager for supporting learning would arrange curriculum release for both coach and coachee in appropriate circumstances. Team coaching was designated to take place on each training day and a neutral coach would be allocated to the team for a year. In most instances, the team would choose the topic, although the leadership team might define a whole-school priority. Individual coaching was voluntary; team coaching was mandatory.

Individual coaching was also made available to maximise the impact of external CPD. The coaching session was designed help the person to identify their learning and construct a plan of action for implementation back at school. A policy decision was made to reduce the extent of external CPD but to give greater coaching support within the implementation phase. This proved very successful. It was also decided to build in a mid-performance management cycle coaching session with a neutral coach (not your performance manager). This initiative was also well received by staff.

The coaching for learning strand was less well developed and a number of initiatives with pupils were piloted.

- *The Year 6 learning project.* This initiative grew out of our reflection on Vivienne's report. The ninety Year 6 children were divided into two matched groups of forty-five: one group would be coached, the other would not, and their SATs scores would be compared at the end of the year. Parents were invited to express a negative preference if they did not want their child to take part—none did. Seven groups of approximately six children were allocated a coach. The children were chosen randomly by their class teachers, with two children from each Y6 class in each mini group. The coaching sessions took place every three weeks and lasted for forty-five minutes. At the end of the year, the coached group did score slightly higher than the control group. However, what was most noticeable was the improvement in their levels of self-esteem. It was decided that in future all Year 6 children would have access to coaching.

- *Transitions.* Coaching was introduced at key points of transition: Year 2 to Year 3, Year 5 to Year 6, and Year 6 to Year 7. The younger children were coached in groups by adults. The Year 6 children were given an abridged coaching course and were asked to coach Year 5 pupils on how to make the most of Year 6. They were also asked to peer coach on the transition to secondary school. The original plan was to have Year 7 students who had attended Hayes Park come back to coach Year 6 children, but this proved impossible to organise. The learning that came from these initiatives was that the children responded in very similar ways to the adults in the school. Most of them enjoyed being coached and found it helpful. A minority were resistant, or just did not understand the process. Some children internalised the approach very quickly and became "born again coaches", and were very evangelistic about the power of the process.
- *Behaviour.* There was an existing body of experience to build on and broaden. The strand manager for supporting learning had been using coaching for some time to help children manage their own behaviour, often at playtimes and lunchtimes. She endeavoured to promote this approach with midday supervisory staff and playground leaders. In addition, she integrated coaching into her wider work: for example, into anger management, relationship issues, and so on. Class teachers and year team leaders also adopted a coaching approach with the children in their charge, encouraging them to take responsibility for their own actions and to develop a proactive approach to solving their own problems.
- *Individual teachers and teaching assistants.* As the coaching culture developed in the school, individuals sought creative ways to maximise the power of coaching for the benefit of the children in their care. A Year 2 teacher developed a picture version of the GROW model and encouraged her pupils to draw their journey. Teaching assistants worked on their listening and question formation. Indeed, coaching with children became a very significant part of existing and future coach development.

We are continuing to develop coaching at Hayes Park. A programme for Teachers' Television (UK) was shot in 2008, four NPQH candidates have undertaken week-long investigations, and four MA students have written dissertations. Many local, national, and international colleagues have visited for varying lengths of time and asked a myriad of questions. The most frequently asked question is: "What advice can you give us about the introduction of coaching at our school?"

My response to the question has developed over the years but still contains the same components.

1.  Be clear about how you want to use coaching in your school. Start from where you are now: your particular context and circumstances and where your school is in its organisational development life-cycle. You might like what you have seen at Hayes Park and you might disapprove of the way some things have been done, but remember it has taken us eight years to get here. Learn from our experience, but translate it into your own context. Building a coaching culture is a long term process—decide where you will make your start.

2.  Building coaching capacity is a key to success. As more people undertook the coach development programme, the quicker the culture took root. It has been said that a thousand details build an impression and the development of a coaching culture involves the coherence of a number of factors. Coaching fits comfortably in an organisation that is committed to shared leadership and demonstrates this in day-to-day action rather than beautifully produced documents. Coaching fits less well in a command and control culture, where, when things go wrong, blame is apportioned to someone else as quickly as possible.

3.  Senior leaders have a key role to play and it is unlikely that coaching will thrive in an organisation where the leaders are not committed to the approach. As the Hayes Park case study demonstrates, the allocation of resources is central to success; the key resources of time, energy, and money need to be committed by the decision makers in the school. Senior leaders also need to "walk the talk" and provide a consistent role model in the way that they coach and are coached. We came to the view that anybody who is coaching should also be coached regularly, including the head teacher. This coaching should be at both the individual and team level.

4.  The workforce remodelling agenda suggested that changes should not involve additional work time for the participants, so

how do we find time for coaching? My response to that question is that coaching should not be a bolt-on activity, but, rather, a strategy for reducing workload by addressing the key challenges in a more systematic and time efficient manner. Coaching could be undertaken as a twilight activity with a high degree of success, but it will probably be even more productive if it is built into the timetabled day. We can be creative about the use of training days, staff meetings, Planning, Preparation, and Assessment (PPA) time and staff curriculum release. My research associate report (Suggett, 2006) was entitled *Time for Coaching* because this is such a key issue!

5.    School-based coaches need ongoing support and encouragement from senior leaders. Effective coaches are an obvious prerequisite of successful coaching. People are likely to be successful if they are trained properly and allocated protected time to do the job. Their training is the start rather than the end of their coaching journey; as indicated above, they need to receive coaching as well as being coaches and they need opportunities to reflect upon their performance and receive high quality feedback. The quality assurance of school-based coaches is a recurring challenge, as the process is confidential and, therefore, continuing professional development arrangements need to be considered.

As we embark upon our next steps, the following summary sets out how we plan to employ coaching in the immediate future.

### Leadership style

A coaching approach to leadership emphasises the importance of asking and listening. On occasions, it is entirely appropriate for leaders at all levels to "tell" rather than to "ask"; good judgement involves knowing when to ask and when to tell. Listening is a greatly underrated leadership skill and both adults and children respond very positively to being listened to! One of our NPQH trainees described us as a "listening school", and we hope to continue to develop this attribute.

Coaching takes an optimistic view of a person's ability to grow and develop and liberates potential. Both coach and coachee grow through the process. A coaching culture has been developed both by design and by default, and new leaders absorb the existing mores of the school. Nevertheless, coaching is only one of a range of leadership styles and it behoves us to be reflective about when it is the right one!

## Coaching for development

The following elements of this strand will continue to be developed.

- Individual coaching on specific opportunities or challenges. This will be arranged when appropriate. For example, a curriculum leader might wish to design an element of our futures curriculum and arrange a series of sessions to work through this process. Alternatively, a teaching assistant might want to develop her listening and questioning skills and enlist the help of a coach.
- Individual coaching as a follow-up to external CPD. For example, this could involve the introduction of a new curriculum initiative or the development of leadership skills learnt on a middle leader programme.
- Individual coaching half way through the performance management cycle. This process enables the coachee to reflect on progress and design the next developmental steps.
- Team coaching for a year group (teachers and teaching assistants) on a topic of your choice with an external coach. Sometimes, the leadership team might define a whole-school initiative, such as preparing for an Ofsted inspection.

## Coaching for learning

The final training day of the past academic year focused on the development of learning coaches as an integral part of constructing the futures curriculum. The immediate plans are as follows.

- Employing a coaching approach with individual learners. The children are very clear about their learning targets and adult and/or peer coaching helps them take responsibility for designing their own learning journey. Each year group had established an action learning project within this context.

- Working with groups of children on a common topic. For example, coaching a group of children who are seeking to improve their writing, and maximising the power of peer coaching within the classroom.
- The teacher using a coaching approach with the whole class. For example, many initiatives within personal and social education have been nurtured using a coaching style.
- Support staff working with individual or groups of children on behavioural issues. This might be a short informal discussion, or a sustained piece of coaching over a designated period of time.
- Coaching for the transitions that were described earlier in the chapter.

All of these coaching for learning initiatives reflect the shared belief that learners should take responsibility for their own learning, and the role of the coach is to ask and not tell. Once again, time is a key consideration, and judgement has to be exercised about value for money and impact.

In conclusion, I believe the impact of coaching at Hayes Park has been profound. It is not a panacea that will solve every problem, but it is a very flexible and versatile tool that, used properly, can add enormous value to any organisation. I am more committed than ever to the coaching process, both as a coach and as a coachee!

## References

Alexander, G. (2006). Behavioural coaching: the GROW model. In: J. Passmore (Ed.), *Excellence in Coaching* (pp. 61–72). London: Kogan Page.

Centre for the Use of Research and Evidence in Education (CUREE) (2005). *National Framework for Mentoring and Coaching*. London: DfES.

Gladwell, M. (2009). *Outliers: The Story of Success*. London: Penguin

Suggett, N. (2006). *Time for Coaching*. Nottingham: NCSL

Whitmore, J. (2002). *Coaching for Performance: Growing People, Performance and Purpose*. (3rd edn). London: Nicholas Brealey.

# CHAPTER ELEVEN

# Coaching students in a secondary school: a case study

*Christian van Nieuwerburgh, Chris Zacharia,
Elaine Luckham, Glenn Prebble, and Lucy Browne*

## Introduction

A collaborative research pilot project between Sittingbourne Community College, educational psychologists within Kent, and the University of East London (UEL) took place in the academic year 2010–2011. Sittingbourne Community College is a large secondary school with over 1,000 students on roll, and nearly half of these students are deemed to experience barriers to learning for a variety of reasons.

The educational psychologists recognised the school's needs and responded with a project proposal for raising attainment using coaching in secondary schools, in line with recent research by Passmore and Brown (2009). Links were then established with the school, and the educational psychologists delivered coaching training to post-sixteen students, supported their interim reflective practice coaching sessions, and helped with the evaluation of the project.

Sittingbourne Community College volunteered to participate in this pilot project, which was consistent with the school's general ethos that considers student voice, leadership, and responsibility as fundamental aspects of a student's education. As such, students of all ages become involved in a variety of ways in working with, and supporting, other students. The College was a leading school in taking forward the Social and Emotional Aspects of Learning (SEAL) strategy so that emotional intelligence is embedded within the curriculum and in interactions between members of the College community.

Secondary school students (post sixteen) were given three days of coaching training and then invited to coach younger students (Year 11) in the school. We were interested in whether coaching (provided by students) could support the standards of achievement and attainment for a selected group of Year 11 students. At the same time, we were curious about the impact of the training and the experience of coaching others on the student coaches themselves. In this case study chapter, we share our initial findings.

## Why coaching?

As stated in the introduction to this book, coaching is a one-to-one conversation focused on the enhancement of learning and development through increasing self-awareness and a sense of personal responsibility, where the coach facilitates the self-directed learning of the coachee through questioning, active listening, and appropriate challenge in a supportive and encouraging climate.

Coaching has traditionally been used with adults in business and sport to enhance performance. More recently, coaching principles and programmes have been used with young people to support examination stress, enhance performance, and promote emotional wellbeing (see Chapter One). As a result, we believed that this approach would support students to take more personal responsibility and increase their own self-awareness, resulting in better examination results.

The GROW model (Whitmore, 2002) was used as the most appropriate coaching framework for this project, based on previous research.

## Aims

There were two aims set for the project. First, to evaluate the coaching training, and second, to look at the impact of the coaching programme on the targeted Year 11 students' GCSE results compared to those of a control group.

## Process

Post-sixteen students (Year 12) were invited to take part in the coaching project to give them additional experiences which could benefit them in their applications to further and higher education. The students were given coaching training, based on the UEL training materials, over the course of three days, by the local authority educational psychologists and staff from the Sittingbourne Community College.

The Year 12 coaches were chosen following previous leadership roles in the school, or because they showed an interest in taking part. Using predictive data for the Year 11 cohort of 2010–2011, fifty equally matched students who were at risk of not achieving five A*–C GCSEs, including English and Maths, were selected as potential recipients of coaching (coachees) for the project. Twenty-five were paired up with the post-sixteen coaches to begin their coaching partnership. The remaining twenty-five students formed the control group, who were offered alternative support if they wished. The final size of the project group comprised eleven coached pairs and a matched control group of eleven young people who were not in receipt of coaching.

The training in coaching commenced in December 2010 and was completed in January 2011. Coaching partnerships were initiated in January 2011, which gave the pairings six months to develop and flourish. An informal approach was given to the pairings, whereby the post-sixteen coaches and Year 11 coachees made their own arrangements to meet up. There were also three interim reflective practice coaching sessions in February, April, and June, in which students were given the opportunity to discuss and share their progress on the coaching so far with the educational psychologists and school staff. By the end of the project, eleven coaching partnerships were sustained and remained effective up until the examination period. This is the figure reflected in the data analysis below.

Finally, the project was reviewed at the end of the formal examinations period, mid-July 2011.

## *Outcomes*

The project was evaluated using both quantitative and qualitative data, with a view to providing a rich picture of student experience and academic results. Questionnaires, semi-structured interviews, and final GCSE results were used to measure outcomes.

### *Evaluation of the coaching training*

Post-sixteen students who undertook the coaching training were asked to complete a questionnaire regarding their confidence pre- and post training on a scale of 1–10 (1 = low confidence, 10 = high confidence). Sixteen out of twenty-five students completed the questionnaires. Three questions were asked in relation to confidence.

1.  How confident do I feel about using coaching as a tool for change?
2.  How confident do I feel about understanding the emotions of others?
3.  How confident do I feel in using a range of study skills?

The results showed that, overall, post-sixteen students who undertook the training felt more confident in the three target areas, as noted below.

"How confident do I feel about using coaching as a tool for change?"

| Before | After |
| --- | --- |
| 4.0 | 7.1 |

This showed that, on average, post-sixteen students reported that following the training, their confidence in using coaching had increased considerably.

"How confident do I feel about understanding the emotions of others?"

| Before | After |
| --- | --- |
| 4.9 | 7.1 |

This showed that there was a similar reported positive effect on the confidence levels of post-sixteen students in the area of understanding the emotions of others following the training.

"How confident do I feel in using a range of study skills?"

| Before | After |
|--------|-------|
| 5.1    | 7.6   |

Students also reported an increase in their ability to use a range of study skills, which was discussed during the training and became one of the main focuses of the coaching conversations.

At the end of the project, further information was obtained from the coaches, coachees, and from members of staff, using questionnaires and semi-structured interviews.

## Feedback from student coaches

The student coaches reported that being involved in the coaching project had been of personal value. This training process had helped them develop new communication and problem-solving skills as well as having some anticipated long-term benefits for future studies/careers, such as enhanced leadership qualities, improved confidence in their ability to think and find their own solutions to problems, and greater independent learning.

The student coaches said that they enjoyed the training, although some wondered whether it would be more manageable if it could be delivered in two days rather than three, thus reducing time out of lessons. Some student coaches found it difficult to engage with their coachee initially, and, in retrospect, would have preferred it if staff had arranged this more formally and systematically. Some student coaches felt that, at times, their relationship with the Year 11 coachee took on a mentoring role. Where this happened, there was agreement that it had been a mutual development between coach and coachee, as it felt more "natural" than coaching.

## Feedback from Year 11 students (coachees)

Those interviewed expressed an appreciation of the supporting nature of the coaching sessions. There was a general consensus that the sessions had been helpful in building confidence and resourcefulness. Several students involved expressed an interest in becoming coaches, as they felt that they had personally benefited from coaching and would like the opportunity to coach younger students. On the other hand, a few coachees said that they did not fully understand why they had been selected for coaching, what coaching entailed, and what the longer-term benefits of being involved in the project would be for them personally.

## Feedback from staff

Staff noted that, during the training sessions, the student coaches were attentive and engaged with the material, suggesting that the training package was appropriate. There was a high level of involvement from all the student coaches in understanding and using the GROW coaching model. Staff were, however, aware that a number of student coaches did not attend all three training sessions due to other college commitments.

## Impact of the coaching programme

In order to measure the academic outcomes of the Year 11 coachees, exam results were collected in the summer of 2011, following the coaching project for both the coached students and the control group. These were arranged into "met or exceeded targets" and "did not meet targets", and the results are shown in (Figure 11.1).

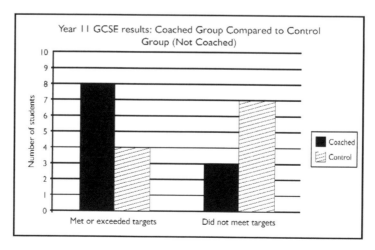

*Figure 11.1.*    Year 11 GCSE results: coached group compared to control group (not coached).

The results show that a larger percentage of coached students (73%) met or exceeded their targets compared with the control group (non-coached students) (36%). Although this result is not statistically significant, due to the small sample size, as an initial finding the outcome is encouraging. Based on this outcome, the college has decided to continue the coaching project for another year.

## Summary and conclusions

The average confidence rating of student coaches following the GROW coaching training was at a level that would support their role as coaches. In addition, they were asked a question about whether they would use coaching in practice following completion of the training programme. Responses indicated that on a scale of 1–10 (1 = low, 10 = high) the average rating was 8.4, showing a willingness and confidence in using the knowledge gained from the coaching training in practice.

The students involved in coaching reported that they enjoyed the experience; 100% of those who completed the questionnaire viewed coaching as a worthwhile activity, 92% wanted to continue the relationship, and 85% reported that they would like to have more sessions. The student coaches, on average, reported increased confidence in using coaching as a tool for supporting younger students. They also reported an increase in their ability to understand emotions (connected to emotional intelligence) and an increased knowledge of a range of study skills.

Additionally, Year 11 coachees, post-sixteen student coaches, and staff identified that the students had responded positively to the programme and developed better self-awareness, interpersonal relationships, and study skills. Areas for development were also identified, which focused on the organisational features of the project, such as the importance of student coaches attending all training sessions and further support from adults on maintaining the momentum of the programme.

Furthermore, data analysis indicates that more students who were coached met or exceeded their academic targets than the control (non-coached) group. Further research with a larger number of young people would help to establish whether an effect could be seen as statistically significant.

*Sharing our learning: suggestions for future
coaching programmes in secondary schools*

1. Staff to offer coachees an introduction to coaching and inform them in advance as to why they have been invited to volunteer, including the benefits for them if they chose to participate.
2. Coachees to be introduced to their coaches prior to starting the sessions, so that they can feel more at ease and, ideally, make a stronger commitment to coaching.
3. Prior to embarking on the coaching programme, full commitment from staff, coaches, and coachees regarding times and venues, etc., should be established.
4. Staff to commit to ongoing interim sessions for coaches, thereby allowing the GROW model to become fully integrated, keeping the focus on coaching as distinct from mentoring.
5. Student coaches could use a logbook to record the logistics of their meetings with younger students and include a reflection on each session to help them articulate to supporting staff what is working and whether further training is required.
6. Careful consideration in the process of selection and commitment of student coaches to reduce the risk of students disengaging from the project due to other commitments.
7. Celebrate successes internally (e.g., certificates in assembly) and publicly.
8. Make the coaching programme an ongoing part of the school's commitment to students. This would also allow for those who had received coaching to become student coaches.
9. Consider inviting all Year 10/11 students to be coached if they wanted, not just those whom either staff or predictive data would suggest might benefit.
10. Undertake further research with larger numbers of young people to help establish a statistically significant effect and wider impact of the coaching programme.

## References

Passmore, J., & Brown, A. (2009). Coaching non-adult students for enhanced examination performance: a longitudinal study. *Coaching: An International Journal of Theory, Practice and Research*, 2(1): 54–64.
Whitmore, J. (2002). *Coaching for Performance: Growing People, Performance and Purpose*. (3rd edn). London: Nicholas Brealey.

# CHAPTER TWELVE

# Coaching staff in a secondary school: a case study

*Loic Menzies*

## Introduction

T his chapter looks at a case study based within a London secondary school, which undertook a pilot programme to investigate how coaching techniques could contribute to staff development. The school is relatively small, with about 600 students aged between 11–16 years. The school caters for a wide range of abilities.

## The pilot

The pilot scheme involved the use of an external coach, who was asked to deliver an hour of coaching to four members of staff at different stages of their career (from newly qualified teacher to experienced manager). In setting up the agreements for each coaching session, the contract on outcomes was left open for the individual to identify their needs, rather than these needs being imposed by the head of department or head teacher.

The feedback from this first set of sessions was positive. The pilot provided some useful insights to what coaching might offer, but it was recognised that for real value to be gleaned from coaching, a wider, whole-school approach was needed.

A wider programme is now under way, and, based on our experiences, we have tried to summarise the key lessons that could be learned from our early experiences of using coaching with secondary school staff.

### Lesson 1: Leave sessions as open as possible

Leaving the objectives open for each session was helpful. Providing a space without determining how that space would be used allowed sessions to go in very different directions: in the pilot phase, one participant chose to focus on developing new teaching and behaviour management strategies, two others focused on their career development, and another concentrated on work–life balance and managing relationships at work. In our experience, coachees welcome the freedom to explore whatever is of most concern to them. This is a notable and welcome difference to traditional personal development reviews, which can tend to focus on departmental and school priorities. By using an external coach and offering flexibility on the topic, the sessions then focus on the key priorities of that individual. This flexibility contributed to the fact that participants in the pilot agreed with the statement, "I enjoyed the session". Furthermore, despite the differing foci of the sessions, all participants agreed with the statement, "I changed something I did as a result of the session".

What was also interesting is that staff in the coaching sessions were interested in the approach and wanted to try it out with their own staff. The effect is that coaching starts to leak out from formal coaching into wider school conversations with staff and with students as the power of the open question is unlocked.

### Lesson 2: Use external expertise to build internal capacity

While it is tempting to read a book and think "that sounds simple", coaching, when done well, is a complex skill. We believe that schools will benefit most from this view if they use an expert to start them on the journey and guide their first few steps. One of the school's senior leadership team, who received training in coaching skills, reported changes to his practice. He had a background in mentoring, but recognised from the training the higher level of skill and expectations required in a coaching conversation. The same benefits came from observing or experiencing coaching, with staff taking from sessions great coaching questions and a new way of working, and offering this to colleagues.

Following the pilot, further data was collected on the experiences of staff. The feedback summarised in Table 12.1 shows the real value of coaching for staff.

*Table 12.1.*   Results of feedback.

| Statement | 1. Disagree strongly | 2. | 3. | 4. Agree strongly | Undecided |
|---|---|---|---|---|---|
| "I found the session useful" | | | 2 | 2 | |
| "I enjoyed the session" | | | 2 | 2 | |
| "I changed something I did as a result of the session" | | | 2 | 2 | |
| "I felt more confident after the session" | 1 | 1 | | 2 | |
| "I felt more motivated after the session" | 1 | 1 | | 2 | |
| "I feel that other staff would benefit from a similar session" | | | 2 | 2 | |
| "A coaching programme would bring benefits to our school" | | | 1 | 2 | 1 |

## *Lesson 3: Gather and share evidence of impact on school improvement*

With many types of initiatives, data is not collected. From our experience, we would suggest that schools collect data right from the start to assess impact. If evidence of impact on school improvement and teacher practice had been systematically gathered, this could be used to apply for further financial resources as well as evidencing the school's journey of learning.

A challenge, however, is how to assess the impact of coaching when goals are so open-ended. In a more fixed outcome approach, the goals for the whole programme can be assessed. An alternative is to consider asking coachees to rate the session and use this as evidence of the usefulness of coaching. However, while this is useful in assessing subjective impact, it cannot evidence impact on teaching and learning, for example. A broader approach is to consider tracking the school's wider progress and comparing its achievements with previous years. This could involve assessing school performance against a dashboard of indicators, from staff development to key examination performance statistics, to measures of social and emotional development of the school. Of course, proving causality through this approach would remain a challenge.

## *Lesson 4: The role of the leadership team*

The role of the leadership team is critical in any change project of this kind within a large organisation. For the pilot coaching programme, staff were told about the project in a staff briefing session. However, most staff were not aware of what was taking place and how they could get involved. Furthermore, at the start of the project, the majority of the leadership team did not understand the aims of the project and, while they were pleased to see it take place, they were not signed up to the full potential that coaching could offer.

Rolling out a coaching programme requires the whole school to "buy in" and for the leadership team to be committed to driving it forward. Specifically, the leadership team needs to have a "coaching champion" who supports and advocates the project. It is also helpful if the wider leadership team actively participates in coaching by having their own coaches or benefiting from coach training, so they are able to use these skills in developing their own staff.

We also hold the view that, by working with the wider staff team, coaching can be viewed as a positive step that is supporting and helping staff, in contrast to a model where coaching is imposed by managers or others and staff are selected based on a deficit model—the worst performers receive coaching. While coaching can help less able teachers to improve and newer teachers make the transition into the school's culture, coaching also has a role to play with experienced and excellent teachers, who can further develop their performance as well as plan how to share these skills with other colleagues for the wider benefit of students and the school.

## Conclusions

While this coaching project has focused on a school starting the journey towards building a coaching culture, we believe we have learnt some useful lessons. Most of all, we have learnt that coaching can be a useful skill for supporting colleagues and can help develop the wider culture of the school towards a learning culture. It is also valuable in that, as staff feedback (above) shows, it is enjoyed and welcomed by staff. This contrasts with more traditional models of INSET. It also remains school based, rather than requiring staff to be sent out on courses, avoiding the cost implications and cover disruption that come with it. Our conjecture, gleaned from staff feedback about how they will apply their learning, also suggests that this approach can lead to a sustainable model in which the school develops the capacity to become self-improving.

# CHAPTER THIRTEEN

# Coaching in higher education: a case study

*Bob Thomson*

I n this chapter, I shall describe a number of ways in which coaching is used at the University of Warwick, and highlight some issues which arise that might be of interest to those seeking to utilise coaching within educational organisations.

In the league tables of British universities that are published regularly, the University of Warwick invariably comes comfortably within the top ten. This is an impressive performance, given that Warwick University was only established in 1964 and, thus, is one of the UK's newer universities. Its strategic vision is to be one of the top fifty universities in the world.

Warwick is a research-intensive university. This is highly significant in shaping how the university is run and has practical implications for both management development and for coaching initiatives. In a research-intensive university, the success of an academic depends largely on the quality of their research publications. The ability to carry out administrative and management duties efficiently, therefore, has a lower priority in their career progression. In some other universities, becoming head of an academic department is seen as a promotion and a step forward in career terms. At Warwick, heads of academic departments are appointed for a fixed term of between three and five years, after which they often return to their former academic role. Heads of academic departments might come to the role at a mid to late stage in their career, with limited prior leadership experience. Being head of department imposes considerable administrative and management responsibilities, all of which take time away from research. The financial recompense for being head of department is modest, and for research-active academics, the vital currency is time rather than money. Hence, becoming head of department can be a burden which people shoulder from a mix of motives, many of which can be rooted in an altruistic desire to "take one's turn" in leading the department.

All these things can pose problems for the efficient running of the university's affairs. On the one hand, the head of department role is a significant management position, while, on the other hand, some people in these roles do not regard themselves as managers and might lack the experience or motivation to develop their leadership skills. In this regard, Warwick is probably no different from other research-intensive universities.

Apart from clients who are academics, there are two other groups of staff at the university who receive coaching. The various administrative departments provide a range of services to support the research and teaching activities of the university. Warwick also has a number of commercial businesses, such as its prestigious conference facilities and the various food and drink outlets around the campus. The administrative and the commercial areas both have more conventional hierarchies, where career progression generally involves taking on greater management responsibilities. Hence, the development of one's management skills is regarded as more relevant and important than is generally the case with academics.

### The Warwick coaching and mentoring scheme

The Warwick coaching and mentoring scheme is open to staff at the university. It has been in operation since 2006, since when, on average, one new coaching or mentoring partnership has been set up each month. The aim of the scheme is to create partnerships, outside the normal line management relationship, where one person helps another to enhance their performance, learning, or development.

A member of staff who is interested in having a coach or mentor, or in being a coach or mentor for someone else, first speaks to their line manager or head of department. This conversation is likely to explore issues such as the reasons why the individual wants to be involved, the time commitment required and how this will be handled, and how the manager might support them. A client's line manager retains a vital role in supporting the development of someone who has an off-line coach or mentor.

Assuming that there is some agreement at this meeting, the next step is to complete a simple, one-page nomination form. The nomination form asks if the respondent would like to have a coach or a mentor, or to act as a coach or as a mentor. It gathers basic information such as job title and grade and contact details, and asks participants what they would like to gain from taking part and what type of person they would like to work with. This helps in matching partners.

The scheme distinguishes between coaching and mentoring. A vital difference between coaching and mentoring concerns the degree to which the coach or mentor guides and directs the client. Within the scheme, coaching sits towards the non-directive end of the spectrum, while mentoring is towards the directive end:

A coach uses their ability to listen and to ask open questions to create a relationship of rapport and trust that enables the other to clarify what matters to them and to work out what to do to achieve their aspirations.

A mentor draws on their experience and knowledge to advise and guide a less experienced person in order to enhance their performance or support their development.

Participation in the scheme is voluntary. Relationships are set up for a fixed duration, generally twelve months, with an end point established at the outset. Some partnerships might continue to meet informally well beyond that time, but this is regarded as outside the scope of the scheme.

Either party may break off the relationship without blame or fault or detailed explanation, and continue in a fresh coaching or mentoring relationship if appropriate.

Coaches and mentors attend an initial one-day workshop to develop the skills and understanding to conduct effective coaching and mentoring conversations and relationships. A coach or mentor has one, or, at most, two, clients at any point in time. A qualified supervisor is available to support a coach or mentor who is concerned about any aspect of their practice.

The scheme is overseen by a programme manager, who keeps a record of participants and facilitates the matching of partners. It has a code of ethics that is based on an adaptation of the Code of Practice published by the European Mentoring and Coaching Council.

## Code of ethics of the Warwick coaching and mentoring scheme

- Coaching and mentoring are confidential activities in which both parties have a duty of care towards each other. The coach or mentor will only disclose information when explicitly agreed with the client or when they believe there is a serious danger to the client or others if the information is withheld.
- Participation—of both parties—is voluntary. Either party may break off the relationship if they feel it is not working. Both parties share responsibility for the smooth winding down and proper ending of their relationship.
- The coach's role is to respond in a non-judgemental and primarily non-directive manner to the client's performance and development needs. The aim is to help the client to articulate and achieve goals. The coach will not impose their own agenda, nor will they intrude into areas that the client wishes to keep off-limits.
- The mentor's role is to understand how the client sees the world, and to offer an appropriate mix of listening and questioning, on the one hand, and advice and guidance, on the other hand, in order to help the client to clarify and achieve performance, development, or career goals. The mentor will not impose their own agenda, nor will they intrude into areas that the client wishes to keep off-limits.
- Both parties will respect each other's time and other responsibilities, ensuring they do not impose beyond what is reasonable. Both parties will also respect the position of third parties.
- The coach or mentor will be aware of, and operate within, the limits of their experience and expertise.
- Both parties will be honest with each other about how the relationship is working.

An important concern about the scheme relates to the level of skills possessed by the coach or mentor. Although some coaches or mentors have well-developed skills (for example, they might have worked as a careers consultant for many years), others start with limited experience of one-to-one work. A one-day training programme in coaching and mentoring skills is necessarily very limited in how far it can develop capability. Within the scheme, supervision is available as a back-up for a coach or mentor, but is not a requirement, and in practice is not utilised very often. Although there have been occasional follow-up days for coaches and mentors, more could have been offered to provide ongoing skills development and reflection on practice. On the other hand, participation in the scheme is voluntary, and those taking part are generally busy people. Introducing requirements such as longer training, regular follow-up days, or mandatory supervision would reduce the number of people willing to act as volunteer coaches or mentors. There needs to be a balance between assuring the quality of the coaching and mentoring, on the one hand, and being realistic about what the coaches and mentors are able to commit to, on the other.

## The Warwick leadership programme

The Warwick leadership programme is open to academic, administrative, and commercial staff with significant leadership and management responsibilities. There are three key elements to the programme. First, there are three one-day workshops where participants explore how they manage themselves and their time, how they lead and manage others, and how they can influence effectively. Second, there are four confidential, one-to-one coaching sessions, for which each participant sets his or her own agenda. This might be to look at a current performance challenge or a difficult working relationship, to develop a particular capability, or to explore future career direction. Third, each participant has the option of receiving 360-degree feedback on his or her leadership style. Typically, between one third and one half of the participants opt to receive 360-degree feedback. The areas covered in the feedback are vision, leading others, planning and monitoring, self-management, influence, and drive. Participants receive ratings on each of these dimensions, together with textual comments in answer to two open questions. These ask what they are particularly good at in leading people, and what they could do more effectively to improve how they lead people.

The mix of workshops and individual coaching sessions is an attempt to balance two things: first, to create a shared experience where a group of diverse people are working together, and, second, to offer a development opportunity tailored to the differing needs of each individual.

One of the great benefits of the programme is the opportunity for people from the academic, administrative, and commercial areas to engage in significant conversation with each other. This networking enables them to appreciate the different challenges and priorities in other areas of the university, and contacts made during the programme can be helpful for many years to come.

Participants vary in their approach to their coaching sessions. Some people hardly engage at all, bringing very little in terms of an agenda they want to work on. Indeed, some participants are up front in saying that there is nothing they would like to be coached on at this time. It is actually better all round if it is agreed to cancel a session rather than to go through the motions. On the other hand, some people derive enormous benefits from their coaching sessions. Some might come back for further sessions years later, while others recommend coaching to their colleagues.

This raises a general question about the effectiveness of coaching as part of a wider management development programme. While someone voluntarily signing up for one-to-one coaching might have some concerns or reservations about what will happen during the coaching, they probably have a fair degree of commitment to the process. Someone signing up for a leadership programme that contains coaching as one aspect of it might be interested in the workshops and the networking opportunities, but be unwilling to be coached on issues facing them. As Gallwey (2000) points out in *The Inner Game of Work*, "coaching cannot be done in a vacuum. If the learner doesn't want to learn, it doesn't make any difference if the coach is a great coach. Coaching is a dance in which the learner, not the coach, is the leader" (p. 207).

## The Warwick coaching network

The Warwick coaching network is a group of members of staff at the university who use coaching in some aspects of their work. The group meets once or twice a year, generally for half a day, followed by a sandwich lunch.

The group has two main purposes. First, as the name indicates, it is a network that provides an opportunity for staff with a working interest in coaching to make contact with one another and hear how people are using coaching in their practice. Members of the network come from different parts of the university, such as the Careers Service, the Business School, the Medical School, and the Institute of Education, and include members of the staff development unit. This leads to a sharing of ideas and, sometimes, to collaborative endeavours. For instance, contacts made through the network led to the Medical School and the Institute of Education working together to develop a postgraduate award in coaching and mentoring.

Second, the group is a community of practice. A member might bring along a model or approach that they use in their work and share this with others, generally by inviting them to engage experientially with the material. As an illustration, one member led the others through an exploration of the use of Edward de Bono's idea of water logic to help them to appreciate the approach and to consider how they might use or adapt it in their own practice. There has also been an interchange of ideas between people in the Careers Service, whose work is mainly focused on students, and other members of the network whose focus is mainly on staff of the university. For example, the Careers Service use a strengths profile, Realise2, to help students to consider their future careers, and have included others in a two-day workshop to learn about the instrument and how it might be used in staff development.

More recently the network has held a number of coaching master-classes. The first looked at solution focused coaching and cognitive–behavioural coaching, and considered how members might incorporate ideas from these two areas in their work. A second master-class explored approaches sitting towards the non-directive end of the coaching spectrum, such as clean language and motivational interviewing.

As well as these two main purposes, one of the benefits felt by members of the network is a sense of support and affirmation for their work and the place of coaching within it. It is heartening to engage with like-minded folk who believe in the value of coaching and who want to extend their coaching capabilities.

## Coaching and mediation

This section considers some of my own work as an internal coach and describes how it is evolving into mediation. A significant part of my role is to offer a confidential, one-to-one coaching service to members of staff of the university. As explained above, this is a key element of the Warwick leadership programme. Apart from this, I coach members of staff on request. The request might come from the individual directly, or it might be a recommendation from the individual's line manager or HR contact that they could benefit from coaching. It sometimes results in a single coaching session, and sometimes leads to a coaching relationship that lasts for several years. Another pattern that is not uncommon is that someone has a number of coaching sessions, and then returns a year or two later for further coaching when something else has emerged that they want to talk through.

There are the usual pros and cons in providing an internal coaching service compared to using external coaches. An obvious benefit is the financial cost. The university needs to meet a salary cost, as opposed to a cost for each coaching session. External coaching is expensive and, other than for very senior people, is beyond the university's budget. Other advantages in offering an internal service include the convenience in meeting locally—the university is housed on a single site on the outskirts of Coventry—and the knowledge the internal coach has of the organisation, its personalities, and its culture. As mentioned in the introduction to this chapter, leadership of academics in a research-led university is very different from management within a more conventional hierarchical structure.

As an internal coach, while confidentiality is part of the contract, it might be that the client or potential client retains doubts about this. Senior people within an organisation might be reluctant to work with an internal coach who is further down the hierarchy, and the nature of their issues might be sensitive or confidential, so that it would be inappropriate to share them with an internal coach. There is also the question of the competence of the coach, and someone working full time as a coach with clients from a variety of organisations and sectors is simply likely to be a better coach, albeit an expensive one.

This coaching service is extending into acting as a mediator within the university. There have been a number of requests to help in situations where there is conflict between two members of staff that threatens to develop into some formal grievance or disciplinary procedure. Such procedures, while necessary, can be very consuming of time and energy, and can be very stressful for those involved. Mediation might be able to facilitate an informal solution that is acceptable to all the parties, thereby avoiding the need to invoke formal processes.

This had led to the creation of a mediation process that offers individuals who are caught up in situations of conflict an informal means of talking through the situation with a neutral party and finding a way forward that enables them to work together with less tension. Participation in the mediation process is voluntary, but those taking part need to be open to the possibility that they might need to change their behaviour. A number of members of staff have successfully completed an accredited programme in workplace mediation.

The role of the mediator is to listen non-judgementally to both parties' points of view; to treat what they are told as confidential; to remain neutral and not take sides; not to adjudicate on what needs to happen next; and not to make recommendations on what should happen next. The mediator structures a number of conversations in order to help the parties, first, to appreciate more deeply each other's perspective and, second, to agree what needs to be done to resolve their conflict with one another.

In many ways, the role of the mediator is similar to that of a non-directive coach, though there is the added complexity that there at least two "clients" involved. The skills involved—such as building rapport, establishing trust, listening non-judgementally, asking open questions, and playing back your understanding—are the same skills that are the basis of good coaching practice.

## What is different about coaching in a university?

This chapter has looked at a number of ways in which coaching is used at the University of Warwick, and highlighted some issues arising. While coaching is increasingly being used in organisations, including other higher education institutions, the chapter has not attempted to describe practice elsewhere in the sector. An interesting question to close with is: *In what ways is coaching in a university different from coaching in other organisations?*

The introduction to this chapter described some aspects of the nature and culture of a research-intensive university. Some of the challenges facing academics—and administrators whose role is to support academics—are different from those facing people employed in a more conventionally hierarchical organisation. It is important in coaching to be aware of this background context. However, while the university context has its special aspects, there are other organisations where there is a group of professional staff who are regarded differently from the support staff: in law firms or hospitals, for example. While it often feels that life is different in the university, many other organisations would equally say that they face unique challenges.

My own view is that coaching in the higher and further education sectors is similar to coaching elsewhere. Clients are dealing with concerns about how they manage themselves and their time, how they relate to colleagues, how they manage staff and their performance, how they influence upwards, and where they are going in their career. These are the issues that people in any organisation might bring to coaching.

## Note

The ideas expressed in this chapter are my own views, and not necessarily those of the University of Warwick.

## Reference

Gallwey, W. T. (2000). *The Inner Game of Work*. New York: Random House.

# INDEX

Abrahamson, E., 31, 43, 108, 111
ACES project, 64, 66
Adams, L., 156, 172
Alexander, G., 178, 190
Allen, D., 79, 83
Allison, S., 15, 21
American Psychological Association, 118
Aristotle, 118
Arthur, J., 149–151
Atkinson, M., 10, 22, 55, 61
Australian Psychological Society, 116
Azadi, K., 89, 91

Bachkirova, T., 6, 14, 21
Backhouse, S. H., 88–89, 91
Bane, K., 124, 131
Barlow, D., 177, 181–182
Bar-On, R., 29, 43–45
Bean, R. M., 56, 61
Berk, L., 134, 151
Bernstein, R. J., 98, 100, 111

Bharwaney, G., 29, 44
Biddulph, S., 141, 151
Biswas-Diener, R., 116–117, 125, 128, 130
Block, P., 98–99, 111
Bloom, G., 28, 31, 35, 44, 95, 111
Bohemia Manor Middle School, 110
Bohm, D., 100, 111
Boudah, D., 97, 112
Boyce, L. A., 58, 60
Bresser, F., 6, 13, 21, 156, 172
Briggs, M., 49–50, 60
Brooks, J., 88, 91
Brouwers, A., 19, 22
Brown, A., 19, 23, 64, 74, 191, 198
Brown, D., 18–19, 21
Brubaker, J. W., 100, 111
Bruen, P., 88, 91
Bruner, J., 142, 151
Buckley, J., 110
Buddha, 118
Bulgren, J., 97, 112

Bull, S., 88, 91
bullying, xviii, 63, 70, 81, 120
Burchinal, M. R., 56, 61
Burton, G., 122, 129
Bush, T., 26, 44

Campbell, D. T., 96, 111
Cantore, S., 162, 172
Career Entry and Development
    Profile (CEDP), 53
Carver, S. M., 49, 61
Case, C. W., 100, 111
case studies
    *Alex*, 147–148
    *Jane*, 143–145
    *Susan*, 145–146
Castagna, C., 28, 31, 35, 44, 95, 111
Cavanagh, M. J., 122, 129, 134, 151
Centre for the Use of Research and
    Evidence in Education (CUREE),
    8, 10, 20–21, 36, 44, 172, 183,
    190
Chafouleas, S. M., 126, 128
Chase Middle School, 96
Christman, J. B., 18–19, 21
Clark, J., 110
Cleese, J., 139, 152
Clonan, S. M., 126, 128
Clough, P. J., 75, 77, 88, 91
Clutterbuck, D., 6, 14, 21, 158, 172
coaching *see also*: self, University of
    Warwick
  academic, 122
  activity, 158
  approaches, 3–4, 9–10, 12–13, 17,
      37, 47, 49, 52, 54, 56–57, 59, 64,
      70, 74, 95, 105, 124–126, 133,
      175–176, 182, 184, 186,
      188–190
  behaviour, 56
  blended, 95
  classroom management, 95
  cognitive–behavioural, 123, 211
  collaborative, 8–10

communities, 8
content-focused, 95
conversations, 10, 13, 35, 60, 68,
    156, 161 162, 195
culture, xix, 20, 29, 37, 58, 124, 126,
    153–165, 167–171, 186–188,
    203
developmental, 123
effective, 3, 27–28, 57, 106, 111, 134,
    155–156, 178, 188, 207, 210
evidence-based, 115–116, 122–123,
    125, 127
evocative, 12, 57
executive, 6, 14, 19, 127
expert, 10
external, 10, 159–160, 189, 199–200,
    212
group, 17, 68–69, 85, 185
high-quality, 9, 29
in education, xvii, xx–xxi, 4, 6–7, 9,
    12, 14, 17–21, 27–28, 38, 90,
    123, 156, 163, 172, 205
informal, 10, 101, 122, 126
initiative, 36, 74, 125, 158, 182, 205
instructional, 12, 17, 47, 49, 55–56,
    61, 95–103, 105, 107–111
internal, 160, 212
interventions, 4, 48, 57, 64, 89,
    127
leadership, 26–27, 36, 38, 123–124,
    188
life, 5, 14, 19, 123
literacy, 12, 56, 95
master-class, 211
models, 4, 27
non-directive, 10, 13, 31, 35, 54
observation, 49
parent, xix, 133–144, 146, 150
peer, 10, 36–37, 48, 50, 64, 69, 95,
    122, 186, 189–190
personal, 19
perspective, 48, 109
practice, 28, 48, 59, 109, 136, 155,
    177–178, 180, 191, 193, 213

process, 42, 86, 96, 175, 183, 190
professional, 19, 64, 66–67, 69, 116, 123
programme, xviii, 3, 8, 37, 56, 64, 67–68, 106, 123, 136, 177, 181, 187, 192, 196, 198, 201–202
project, 71, 193, 195–197, 203
psychology, xix, 115–117, 121–124, 126–128
pupil, 10, 179
relationship, 17, 58, 69, 73, 101–103, 110, 125, 155, 212
session, 18, 37, 40–42, 66, 69, 73, 171, 177–179, 181, 184–185, 191, 193, 195, 199–200, 209–210, 212
skill, 4, 9, 16, 20, 27–28, 36–37, 47, 49–51, 64, 66–69, 71, 134, 136, 138, 142, 144, 146–148, 150, 160, 201
specialist, 8–11
sports, 14, 86
strengths-based, 127
style, 10, 29–30, 36, 190
team, 10, 178–180, 184–185, 189
technique, xx, 199
Codding, R., 122, 130
Cohen, S., 109–110
Collins, J., 154, 171–172
Connaughton, D., 88–89, 91
continuing professional development (CPD), 4, 8–9, 57, 184–185, 188–189
Contreras, Y. M., 123, 128
Cornett, J., 94, 97, 112
Covey, S., 99, 112
Cox, E., 6, 14, 21
Creasy, J., 9, 20–21, 27, 29, 34, 44, 153–154, 172
Crust, L., 89, 91
Curtayne, L., 122, 129

Darnon, C., 119, 131
Dean, B., 117, 128

Deci, E. L., 122, 128, 132
de Haan, E., 6, 14, 21, 28, 44, 157, 172
Dembkowski, S., 6, 21
Denton, C., 123, 128
Department for Children, Schools and Families (DCSF), 5, 9, 21
Department for Education, 5, 22
Department for Education and Skills (DfES), xviii, 7, 22
Deshler, D. D., 97, 112
Devine, N., 110
Dewey, J., 5–6, 22
Diamond, K. E., 56, 61
DiClemente, C. C., 122, 131
Dobie, S., 58, 60
Doran, J., 122, 129
Downey, M., 14, 22
Driel, J., 52, 61
DuFour, R., 107, 112
Duijts, S. F. A., 122, 128
Dunn, J., 135, 151
Dweck, C. S., 137–138, 151

education(al) *see also*: coaching
    attainment, xviii, 12, 63
    colleges, 37
    community, xix, xxi, 36
    contexts, 4, 18, 31, 39–41, 43, 49
    elementary, 48–49
    environment, 89
    excellence, 5
    experiences, 5, 20–21, 51
    further, xviii, xx, 47, 214
    higher, xvii, xx, 53, 79, 83, 119, 193, 213
    institutions, 20
    leader(ship), 3–4, 20, 25–27, 29–32, 34–38, 40, 42–43, 123
    organisation, xix, 3–4, 7, 12–14, 20–21, 27, 29, 31, 37, 40, 47–48, 58, 150, 154, 156, 163, 167–168, 205
    persona, 38–43

practitioners, 36
primary, xvii–xviii, 49, 51
professionals, 7, 36, 40, 58
programme, 115, 118, 120, 124,
    127
psychology, xx, 68, 120, 191, 193
role, 41
secondary, 35, 47, 51, 87
sector, 35, 49, 122
special needs, 51, 180
systems, 4–5, 20, 35
theory, 11
workforce, 37
*Educational Leadership*, 12, 22
Edwards, D., 52, 60
Eisengart, S., 122, 129
Eisler, R., 98, 112
Eldridge, F., 6, 21
Elias, M. J., 29, 44
Elish-Piper, L., 56, 61
Emmons, R. A., 119, 129
Ernst, R., 121, 131
European Mentoring and Coaching
    Council, 208
Evers, W. J. G., 19, 22

Faber, A., 139, 151
Fitzsimmons, G., 26, 30, 44
Fontana, A., 96, 112
Fordyce, M. W., 120, 129
Franklin, J., 122, 129
Freedman, J. L., 139, 151
Freire, P., 98, 100, 112
Frey, J. H., 96, 112
Fullan, M., 43–44, 98, 107, 112
Furlong, M., 120, 129
Furnham, A., 26, 44

Gable, S. L., 117, 129
Gallwey, W. T., 14, 22, 210, 214
Garcea, N., 125, 130
Gardiner, W., 54, 61
Garvey, R., 13, 22
Geelong Grammar, 120, 124, 126

Gillett, R., 116, 130
Gillham, J., 121, 131
Gilman, R., 120, 129
Gingerich, W., 122, 129
Gladwell, M., 182, 190
Golawski, A., 138, 151
Goleman, D., 29–30, 44
Grainger, T., 149–151
Grant, A. M., 6, 19, 22–23, 116–117,
    122–123, 125, 127, 129–130, 132,
    134, 151
Green, L. S., 19, 22, 122–123, 125, 127,
    129–130
Grenny, J., 102, 112
Gross-Cheliotes, L., 13, 22
GROW coaching model, 68, 178–179,
    181, 186, 192, 196–198
Guise, S., 26, 30, 44
Guldberg, H., 133, 135, 141–142,
    151

Haidt, J., 117, 129
Hall, G. E., 107, 112
Hanton, S., 88–89, 91
Harbour, M., 15, 21
Harrington, S., 117, 125, 130
Hart, B., 138, 151
Hartley-Brewer, E., 138, 151
Hasbrouck, J., 123, 128
Hawkins, P., 6, 22
Hayes Park, 176–177, 182–183,
    186–187, 190
    coaching strategy, 180
    Primary School, xx, 59, 124, 154,
    186
Holt, J., 142, 151
Homer, 13
Hord, S. M., 107, 112
Horsburgh, V., 87, 91
Houghton-Mifflin reading
    programme, 110
Howson, J., 34, 44
Huebner, E. S., 120, 123, 129–130
Hugh, R., 18–19, 21

Huitt, W., 119, 130
Hunter, I., 6, 21

Ingham, H., 38, 44
Isaacs, W., 98, 112

Jackson, R. J., 58, 60
Jacobson, L., 19, 23, 138, 151
James, W., 88, 91
Jastrzebska, K., 158–159, 172
Jeffreys, M., 5, 22
Johari's Window, 38, 40, 42, 44
Jones, G., 88–89, 91
Joseph, S., 118, 130

Kaiseler, M., 89, 91
Kansas Coaching Project (KCP),
    95–99, 101, 103, 106–107, 109
Kant, I., 122, 128
Kauffman, C., 117, 130
Kegan, R., 105, 112
Kemp, T., 127, 130
Killion, J. P., 100, 112
Kline, N., 138, 151
Knight, J., 12, 22, 56, 61, 93–97,
    101–102, 112–113
Kobasa, S. C., 76, 91
Koehler, M. J., 56, 61
Kolb, D., 125, 130
Kopelman, R., 124, 131

Lahey, L., 105, 112
L'Allier, S., 56, 61
Lawrence-Lightfoot, S., 99, 112
Layard, R., 135, 151
Lenz, B. K., 97, 112
Levy, A. R., 88–89, 91
Lewis, S., 162, 172
Linkins, M., 121, 131
Linley, P. A., 116–118, 125, 130
Loehr, J. E., 76, 91
London Institute of Education,
    184
Lord, P., 10, 22, 55, 61

Lucas, B., 140, 151
Luft, J., 38, 44
Lyubomirsky, S., 117–120, 132

Machin, S., 51, 61
MacKinlay, A., 29, 44
Macquarie University, 123
Madden, W., 19, 22, 125, 130
Maree, J. G., 29, 44
Matheson, D., 138, 151
Maxfield, D., 102, 112
Mazlish, E., 139, 151
McDougal, J. L., 126, 128
McGrath, H., 120, 130–131
McKale, T., 95, 113
McKnight, C. G., 123, 130
McMillan, R., 102, 112
McNally, S., 51, 61
Megginson, D., 13, 22, 158, 172
Meghir, C., 51, 61
mental toughness, xviii–xix, 75–77,
    79–90
    questionnaire (MTQ48), 75, 77–78,
        80–81, 83–86, 88–90
mentor(ing), 3, 8–11, 13–16, 20, 25, 27,
    31, 35–36, 51–55, 59, 69, 73–75,
    84–85, 90, 157–158, 179, 183, 195,
    198, 201, 206–209, 211
    learning, 14, 51–52
    peer, 54
    programme, 8, 14
    relationship, 73
    skills, 53, 209
Mercer, N., 52, 60
*Merriam–Webster Dictionary*, 14, 23
Merriman, D., 122, 130
Mintz, J., 51, 61
Mitchell, H., 10, 22, 55, 61
Moir, E., 28, 31, 35, 44, 95, 111
Moxley, D. E., 12, 23
Mueller, C. M., 137, 151

National Assessment of Educational
    Progress (NAEP), 94

National Association of Head
    Teachers, 34
National College for School
    Leadership (NCSL), 9, 29, 34,
    153–154, 182
National Commission on Excellence
    in Education, 119, 131
National Foundation for Educational
    Research (NFER), 10
National Framework for Mentoring
    and Coaching, 8–11, 15, 183
Neal, L. J., 58, 60
Newton, S., 88, 91
Nicholls, A. R., 88–89, 91
Nielsen, A. M., 116, 130
Nilsson, P., 52, 61
Nineteen Minutes, 136–137
Noble, T., 120, 131
Nolan, M. E., 14, 23
Norrish, J. M., 119, 121, 131

Oades, L. G., 19, 22, 122, 127, 130
Olivero, G., 124, 131
Oxford English Dictionary (OED), 14,
    23, 98

Palmer, P., 100, 112
Palmer, S., 142, 151
Parent Gym, 136
Park, N., 118, 120, 131
Parker, H., 122, 129, 134, 151
Parker, J. D. A., 29, 44
Passmore, J., 6, 15, 19, 23, 27, 45, 64,
    74, 122, 129, 134, 151, 158–159,
    162, 172, 191, 198
Paterson, F., 9, 20–21, 27, 29, 34, 44,
    153–154, 172
Patterson, K., 102, 112
Peltier, B., 6, 23
Penn Resiliency Programme, 126
Perks, J., 29, 45
Peterson, C., 118, 120–121, 131
Plumer, P. J., 123, 131
Polman, R. C., 88–89, 91

Poortvliet, P. M., 119, 131
Porritt, V., 184
positive psychology, xix, 20, 76,
    115–128
Powell, D. R., 56, 61
Prochaska, J. O., 122, 131

Reagan, J. G., 100, 111
Reilly, M. F., 13, 22
Reinke, W., 95, 113
Reivich, K., 121, 131
Reumann-Moore, R., 18–19, 21
Riffer, M., 18–19, 21
Riley-Tillman, T. C., 126, 128
Risley, T., 138, 151
Rivers, J. C., 94, 113
Robbins, B. D., 118, 131
Robertson, J., 36, 45
Robins, L., 58, 60
Rosenthal, R., 19, 23, 138, 151
Ross, J. A., 18, 23
Rumsfeld, D., 38–39, 42
Ryan, R. M., 122, 128, 132
Rynsaardt, J., 19, 22, 122–123,
    129

Salmon, P., 141, 151
Sanders, W. L., 94, 113
Santrock, J., 135, 151
Schermer, J., 87, 91
Schön, D. A., 100, 135
Schumaker, J., 97, 112
self
    -assessment, 50, 162
    -awareness, 17, 20, 27, 37, 41–42,
        63, 136, 157, 192, 197
    -belief, 79, 138
    -changing, 157
    -coaching, 10, 70
    -confidence, 16, 32–33, 37
    -destruction, 119
    -determination, xviii, 58, 122
    -development, 78
    -discipline, 138

-efficacy, 19
-esteem, 16, 18, 32, 58, 120, 134,
    156, 183, 185
-evident, 176
hidden, 38–39, 41–42
-improvement, 57, 203
-management, 209
monitor, 55
-reflection, 10, 20, 136, 143, 156
-regard, 27
-regulation, 116
-responsibility, 141
-selected, 57–58
-talk, 89
-transcendent, 119
-understanding, 157
Seligman, M. E. P., 118, 120–121,
    131
Senge, P., 98, 100, 113
Sergiovanni, T. J., 37, 45
Shambrook, C., 88, 91
Sheldon, K. M., 118, 122, 132
Shidler, L., 19, 23
Showers, B., 95, 113
Simon, H., 52, 61
Sin, N. L., 117–120, 132
Sittingbourne Community College,
    xx, 191, 193
Skynner, R., 139, 152
Smith, L. C., 123, 130
Smith, N., 6, 22
Smith, S., 58, 60
Spence, G. B., 19, 23, 122, 127, 132
Spokane Public School, 55, 61
Sprick, R., 95, 109, 113
Sprigade, A., 34, 44
Stanley, J. C., 96, 111
Starr, J., 140, 152
Starratt, R. J., 37, 45
Staub, F. C., 95, 113
Steen, T., 118, 120, 131
Steiner, R., 139–140, 152
Stiggins, R., 109
Stokes, P., 13, 22

Stoner, G., 123, 131
StrathHaven Positive Psychology
    Curriculum, 126
Sturtevant, E. G., 12, 23
Suggett, N., 9, 188, 190
Suldo, S. M., 123, 130
Swaen, G. M. H., 122, 128

Taylor, P. R., 36, 45
Taylor, R. T., 12, 23
Teacher Development Agency, 53,
    61
Thomas, L., 135, 152
*Time Use Survey*, 135, 152
Todnem, G. R., 100, 112
Toll, C. A., 12, 23
Tomic, W., 19, 22
Training and Development Agency
    for Schools, 10, 23
Trosten-Bloom, A., 162, 172
Tschannen-Moran, B., 12, 23, 57,
    61
Tschannen-Moran, M., 12, 23, 57,
    61

Universal Declaration of Human
    Rights, 5
University of East London (UEL), xx,
    191
University of Modena and Reggio, 88
University of Parma, 88
University of Warwick, xx, 205–6,
    213–214
    coaching and mentoring scheme,
        206, 208
    coaching network, 210
    leadership programme, 209, 212
University of Western Ontario, 87

van den Brandt, P. A., 122, 128
van Nieuwerburgh, C., 49–50, 60
Vella, J., 100, 113, 119, 121, 131
Vella-Brodrick, D. A., 119, 121, 131
Venneri, A., 88, 91

Vernon, P., 87, 91
Veselka, L., 87, 91
Vlach, H. A., 49, 61

Warren, B., 28, 31, 35, 44, 95, 111
Wearmouth, J., 141, 152
Wenglinsky, H., 94, 113
West, L., 95, 113

Whitmore, J., 13–14, 20, 23, 68, 74,
    178, 190, 192, 198
Whitney, D., 162, 172
Wilson, A., 136, 141, 152
Wilson, C., 6, 13, 21, 156, 172
Wiseman, R., 137, 152
Wong, P. T. P., 119, 132
Wray, D., 149–151